aftermath

DALE
SEYMOUR

Palo Alto,
California

MARY LAYCOCK
Nueva Learning
Center
Hillsborough,
Calif.

VERDA HOLMBERG
Mt. Diablo U.S.D.
Concord,
Calif.

BOB
LARSEN
Cartoonist

Ruth
HELLER
Designer

ISBN: 0-88488-033-8

7 8 9 10 11 12 . 8 9 8 7 6 5 4 3

A PUZZLE PAGE FOR TEACHERS

WHAT IS THE ANSWER TO THESE QUESTIONS?*

* TO FIND THE ANSWER, ORDER THE LETTERS BY THE QUESTIONS TO FORM ONE WORD.

OKAY...NOW HOW DO I **AFTERMATH?**

DEDICATION:

THIS BOOK IS
DEDICATED TO COL.
ROBERT S. BEARD. HIS
INSIGHTS INTO THE BEAUTY
OF MATHEMATICS HAVE BEEN
A GREAT INSPIRATION TO
THE AUTHORS OF THIS
BOOK AS WELL AS
MANY OTHERS.

ACKNOWLEDGEMENTS:

JUDY WILLIAMSON

REUBEN SCHADLER

DENNIS HOLMAN

CAROL CASHIN

FRAN WUNDER

FRED HORNBRUCH

BILL JUAREZ

EARLY GREEK AND ROMAN BANKERS MADE AN ABACUS OF **STONE**. IT HAD **GROOVES** IN WHICH THE CALCULI MOVED.

THAT'S GROOVY!

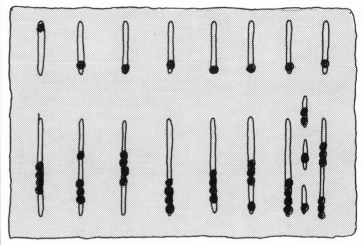

ANCIENT ROMAN ABACUS

DON'T THE **CHINESE** AND **JAPANESE** USE THE ABACUS TOO?

CHINESE, JAPANESE, RUSSIANS, AND MANY OTHER PEOPLES HAVE USED THE ABACUS FOR CENTURIES. SOME PEOPLE CAN CALCULATE FASTER ON AN ABACUS THAN OTHERS CAN CALCULATE ON AN ADDING MACHINE.

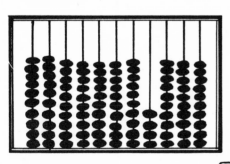

RUSSIAN ABACUS (S'CHOTY)

CHINESE ABACUS (SUAN PAN)

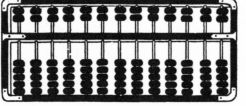

JAPANESE ABACUS (SOROBAN)

2

THE RODS UP AND DOWN REPRESENT PLACE VALUE. UNITS, TENS, HUNDREDS, ETC.

THOUSANDS
HUNDREDS
TENS
UNITS

THE JAPANESE ABACUS (SOROBAN) HAS ONE BEAD ON THE TOP FRAME. THIS REPRESENTS FIVE OF THAT PLACE VALUE. EACH BEAD ON THE BOTTOM REPRESENTS ONE OF THAT PLACE VALUE.

5 EACH

1 EACH

HERE'S HOW TO COUNT ON THE ABACUS.

ONE TWO THREE FOUR FIVE SIX

SEVEN EIGHT NINE TEN ELEVEN TWELVE THIRTEEN FOURTEEN

CAN YOU SOLVE THIS ABACUS PUZZLE?

GIVE THE NUMBER NAMED ON THE ABACUS IN EACH PROBLEM
BELOW, THEN USE THE CODE TO FIND THE MESSAGE.

ODD	D	O	T	R	U	S	N	EVEN	Y	O	U	P	L	S	A	B	C
PROBLEMS	4	2	8	1	9	3	7	PROBLEMS	6	1	5	9	7	2	3	8	4

1

2

3

4

5

6

3

WHICH ONE DIFFERS?

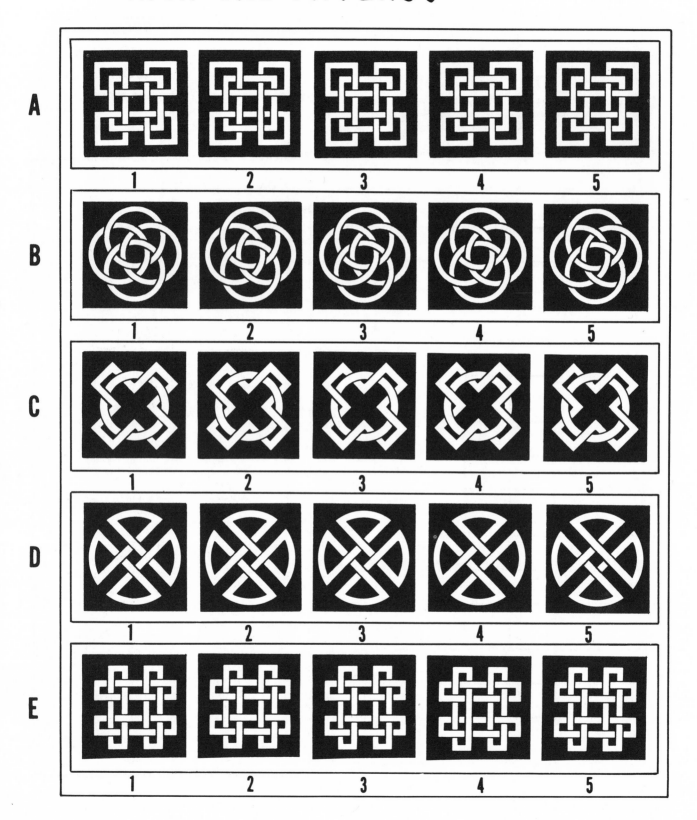

MATH PUN FUN

UNSCRAMBLE THE FIVE MATH WORDS BELOW, WRITING EACH IN ITS SPECIAL BOX. TRANSFER THE LETTERS IN THE NUMBERED SQUARES TO THE BLANKS IN THE JOKE AT THE RIGHT!

LAHF

H	A	L	F
4			

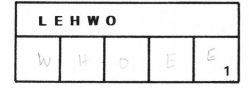

LEHWO

W	H	O	E	E
				1

TIGEH

E	H	G	A	T
		3		

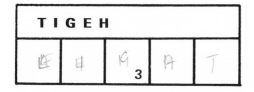

CAMIDEL

D	E	C	I	M	A	L
			2			

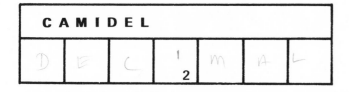

TARNIFCO

F	R	A	C	T	I	O	N
				5			

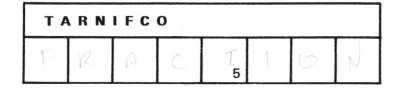

5

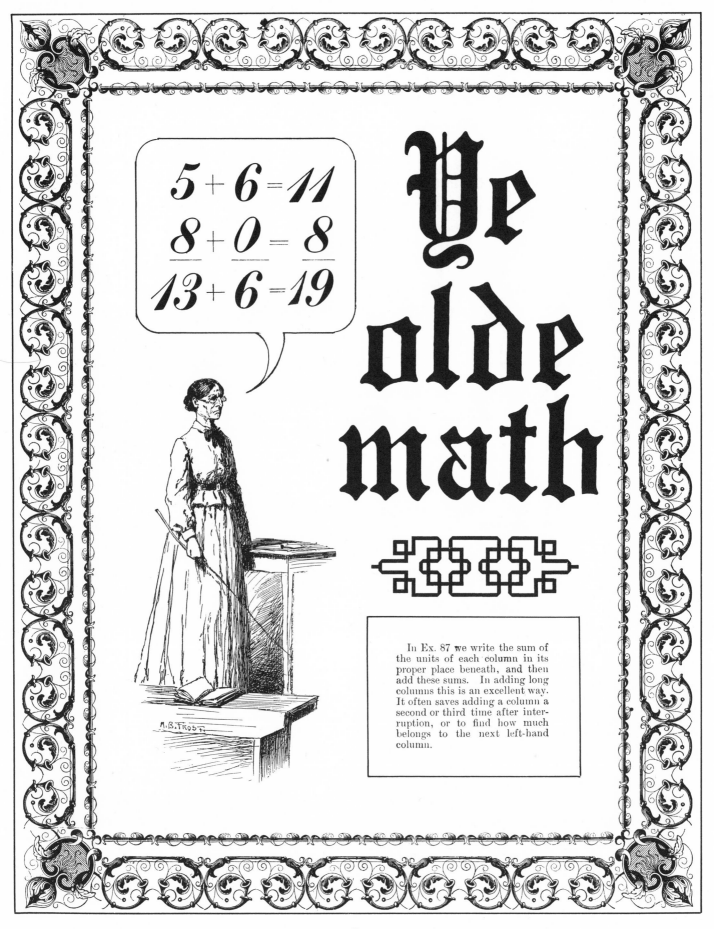

Ye olde math

In Ex. 87 we write the sum of the units of each column in its proper place beneath, and then add these sums. In adding long columns this is an excellent way. It often saves adding a column a second or third time after interruption, or to find how much belongs to the next left-hand column.

58. On one tree were 17 pears, on another 426, on another 302, and on another 213. How many pears were there?

59. One farmer has 643 sheep, another has 529, and another has 375. How many have they all?

60. Mr. Atwood has 393 dollars in the bank, Mr. Jones has 539 dollars, and Mr. Johnson has 615 dollars. How much have they in the bank?

61. A locomotive went 118 miles one day, 197 another, 236 another, and 183 another. How far did it go?

27. ORAL EXERCISES.

62. What is the sum of 5, 7, 9, 8, and 4?

63. A boy paid 18 cents for a top, 5 cents for a pencil, 6 cents for oranges, and 9 cents for writing-paper. How many cents did he pay for all?

64. A farmer sold 3 bushels of potatoes to one man, 17 to another, 5 to another, and 8 to another. How many bushels did he sell?

65. John collected for his father 8 dollars from one man, 6 dollars from a second, 3 dollars from a third, and 7 dollars from a fourth. How many dollars did he collect?

66. James paid 35 cents for an arithmetic, 8 cents for a writing-book, 5 cents for a lead-pencil, and 9 cents for ink. How many cents did he pay for all?

67. A grocer sold a pound of cheese for 11 cents, a pound of crackers for 10 cents, and a pound of sugar for 9 cents. How many cents' worth did he sell?

68. A farmer has 12 acres of corn, 6 acres of wheat, 4 acres of rye, and 3 acres of oats. How many acres of grain has he?

69. In a certain orchard there are 23 apple-trees,

ALL WAYS

IN THE FIGURE AT THE RIGHT, THE SEVEN PAIRS OF ADJACENT SQUARES HAVE SEVEN DIFFERENT SUMS.

4	5	6
9	7	8

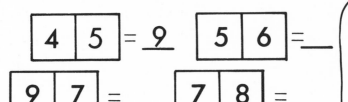

| 4 | 5 | = 9 | | 5 | 6 | = __ |

| 9 | 7 | = __ | | 7 | 8 | = __ |

HE MEANS THAT THESE SEVEN DIFFERENT COMBINATIONS GIVE SEVEN DIFFERENT SUMS.

4
9
___
13

5
7
___

6
8
___

PLACE THE NUMERALS 1, 2, 3, 4, 5 AND 6 IN THE SQUARES BELOW TO GIVE SEVEN DIFFERENT SUMS LIKE THE PUZZLE ABOVE.

YOU'LL NEED A PENCIL WITH A GOOD ERASER.

OR ELSE CUT OUT SIX SQUARES SO YOU CAN MOVE THEM AROUND.

HOW MANY DIFFERENT SOLUTIONS CAN YOU AND YOUR CLASSMATES FIND FOR THIS PUZZLE?

GUESSTIMATES

SOMETIMES PEOPLE HAVE MISUNDERSTANDINGS BECAUSE THEY DON'T ESTIMATE CLEARLY IN NUMBERS.

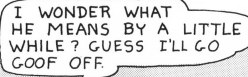

DON'T USE PHRASES LIKE:

— I'LL BE THERE SHORTLY.	TIME
— IT'S JUST A SHORT DRIVE.	DISTANCE
— OH, THERE AREN'T VERY MANY.	NUMBERS
— HE'S REALLY OLD.	AGE

CAN YOU THINK OF ANYMORE?

_____

_____

_____

_____

9

GUESSTIMATES

WHICH OF THE THREE ESTIMATES IS CLOSEST?

(DON'T COUNT.)

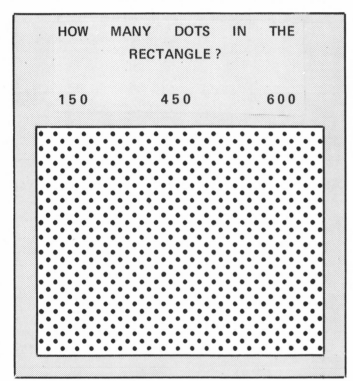

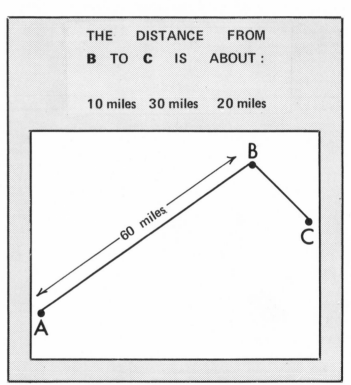

10

THERE ARE THE SAME NUMBER OF TALLY MARKS IN BOX 1 AND BOX 2 BELOW.

HOW MANY TALLIES IN EACH BOX?

OBJECTS ARE EASIER TO COUNT IF THEY ARE ARRANGED IN A PATTERN.

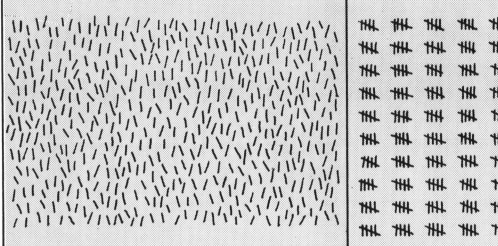

BOX 1

BOX 2

WHICH BOX DID YOU CHOOSE TO COUNT?

BOX **2**, I HOPE.

DID YOU COUNT EVERY SINGLE TALLY OR DID YOU USE A SHORT CUT?

WAS IT NECESSARY TO COUNT THE TALLIES IN BOTH BOXES?

I THOUGHT: 5 IN EACH "BUNCH", 10 BUNCHES TO A ROW,... THAT'S 50 TO A ROW AND THERE ARE 10 ROWS, SO THAT IS 50 X 10 OR 500 MARKS.

SMARTY!

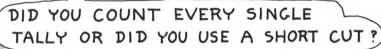

11

GUESSTIMATES

FIND THE NUMBER OF OBJECTS ON THIS PAGE WITHOUT
COUNTING EVERY OBJECT. LOOK FOR PATTERNS.

A

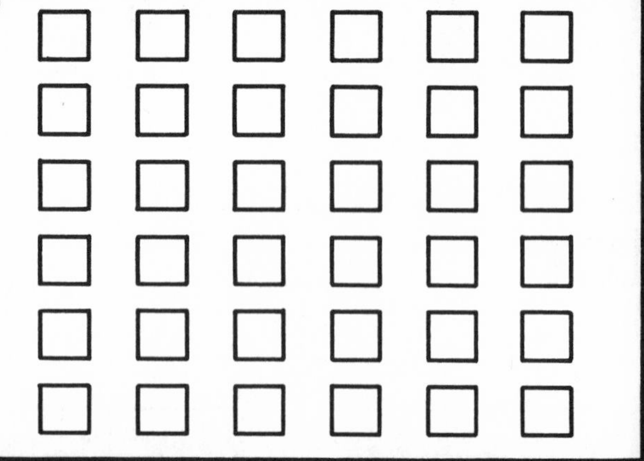

B

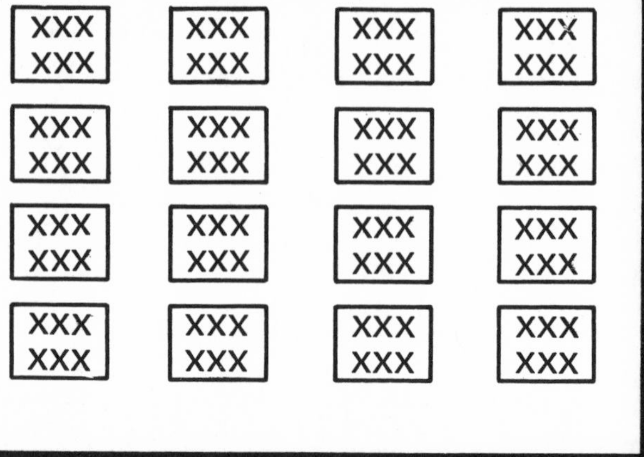

C COUNT ALL THE O's

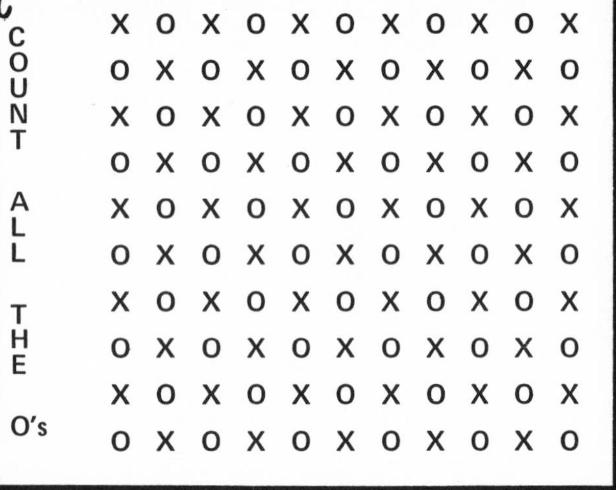

D

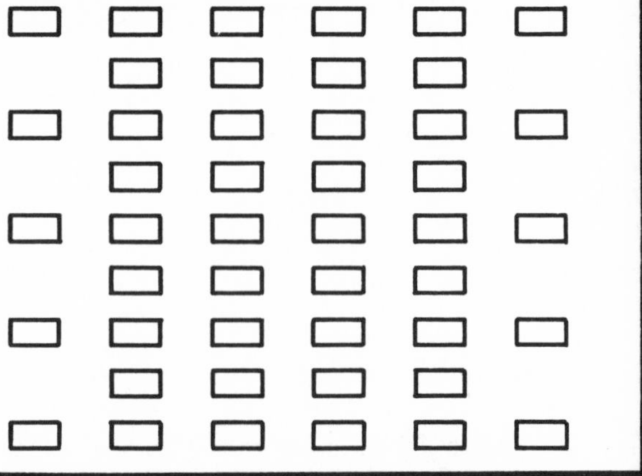

E

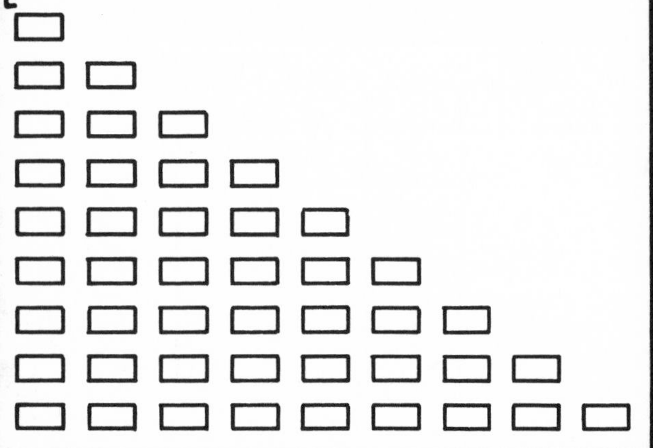

F COUNT ALL CIRCLES

12

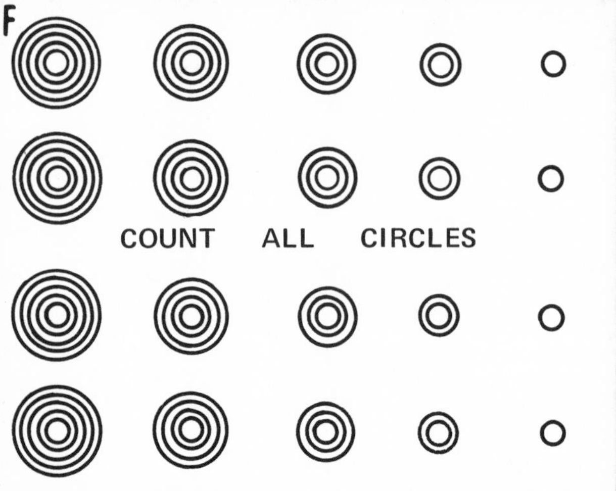

EVEN AND ODD

COMPLETE:

EVEN | ODD

+	2	4	6	8
2				
4				
6				
8				

×	2	4	6	8
2				
4				
6				
8				

+	1	3	5	7
1				
3				
5				
7				

×	1	3	5	7
1				
3				
5				
7				

+	O	E
O		
E		

×	O	E
O		
E		

13

ODD AND EVEN MAZE

FIND A PATH OF EVEN BLACK NUMERALS LEADING INTO THE CENTER. FIND A PATH OF ODD WHITE NUMERALS LEADING INTO THE CENTER.

14

NUMERALS-PAST AND PRESENT

	ZERO	ONE	TWO	THREE	FOUR	FIVE	SIX	SEVEN	EIGHT	NINE	TEN
BABYLONIAN CUNIFORM		∨	∨∨	∨∨∨	∨∨∨∨	∨∨∨∨∨	∨∨∨∨∨∨	∨∨∨∨∨∨∨	∨∨∨∨∨∨∨∨	∨∨∨∨∨∨∨∨∨	◁
EGYPTIAN HIEROGLYPHICS		∕	∕∕	∕∕∕	∕∕∕∕	∕∕∕∕∕	∕∕∕∕∕∕	∕∕∕∕∕∕∕	∕∕∕∕∕∕∕∕	∕∕∕∕∕∕∕∕∕	∩
MAYAN NUMERALS		⊖	⊖⊖	⊖⊖⊖	⊖⊖⊖⊖	—	⊖	⊖⊖	⊖⊖⊖	⊖⊖⊖⊖	=
GREEK ALPHABET NUMERALS		A′	B′	Γ′	Δ′	E′	F′	Z′	H′	θ′	I′
ROMAN NUMERALS		I	II	III	IV	V	VI	VII	VIII	VIIII	X
HINDU BRAHMI		—	=	≡	⅄	┣	6	7	ς	?	α
HINDU GWALIOR	o	૧	૨	૩	૪	૫	૬	૭	૮	૭	•
MODERN CHINESE		～	≈	≋	四	五	六	七	八	九	十
GOTHIC		A	B	Γ	∂	Є	ᴜ	Z	ᴧ	Ψ	ⅱ
HEBREW		א	ב	ג	ד	ה	ו	ז	ח	ט	י
ARABIC		١	٢	٣	٤	٥	٦	٧	٨	٩	٠

15

ADD-SUB SLIDE RULE

EVER SEEN A **SLIDE RULE**, JEFF?

YEAH! MY DAD'S GOT ONE.

DIRECTIONS BELOW SHOW YOU HOW TO MAKE A SIMPLE **SLIDE RULE** OF YOUR OWN.

FIRST: CUT OUT THE SLIDE **A** AND THE FOLDER **B**.

| 0 | 1 | 2 | 3 | 4 | 5 | 6 | 7 | 8 | 9 | 10 | 11 | 12 | 13 | 14 | 15 | 16 | 17 | 18 |

SLIDE A

| 0 | 1 | 2 | 3 | 4 | 5 | 6 | 7 | 8 | 9 | 10 | 11 | 12 | 13 | 14 | 15 | 16 | 17 | 18 |

FOLD ON DOTTED LINE

FOLDER B

SECOND: FOLD BACK FOLDER **B** ON THE DOTTED LINE.

THIRD: PLACE SLIDE **A** INSIDE FOLDER **B**. THE NUMBER LINE **A** APPEARS ABOVE THE NUMBER LINE ON **B**. ON THE NEXT PAGE WE WILL SHOW YOU HOW TO USE THE SLIDE RULE. ➔

ADD-SUB SLIDE RULE

PROBLEM: 3 + 2 = **N**

1.   PULL   SLIDE   **A**   UNTIL   **O**   IS   OVER   **3**
     ON   FOLDER   **B**.

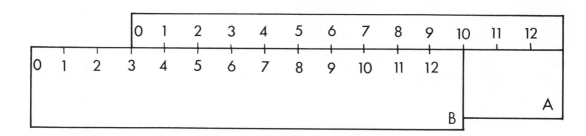

2.   ON   SLIDE   **A**   FIND   **2**.   THE   ANSWER
     N   IS   UNDER   **2**.   **N** = _____

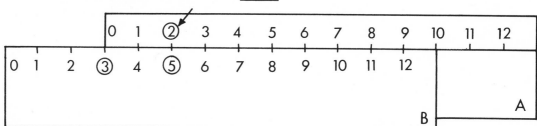

HEY! THAT'S EASY. LET ME TRY.

OK, TRY THESE PROBLEMS.

$7 + 5 = N$
$9 + 4 = N$
$2 + 7 = N$
$8 + 7 = N$
$4 + 1 = N$
$3 + 0 = N$

(CONTINUED)

17

ADD-SUB SLIDE RULE

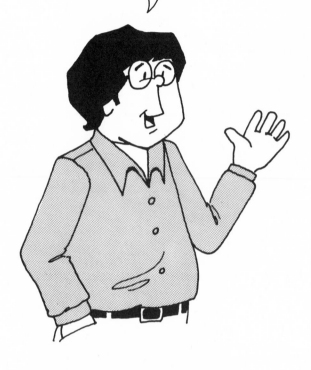

HERE'S HOW TO SUBTRACT ON THE ADD-SUB SLIDE RULE.

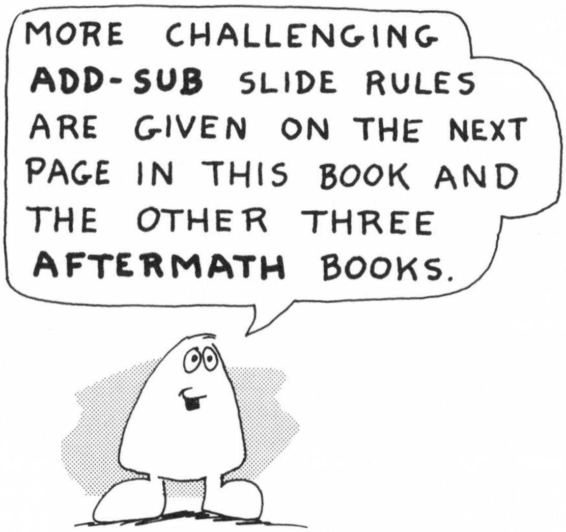

PROBLEM: **5 − 3 = N**

1. PULL THE SLIDE **A** UNTIL **0** IS OVER **3** ON FOLDER **B.**

A
0 1 2 3 4 5
0 1 2 3 4 5 6 7 8
B

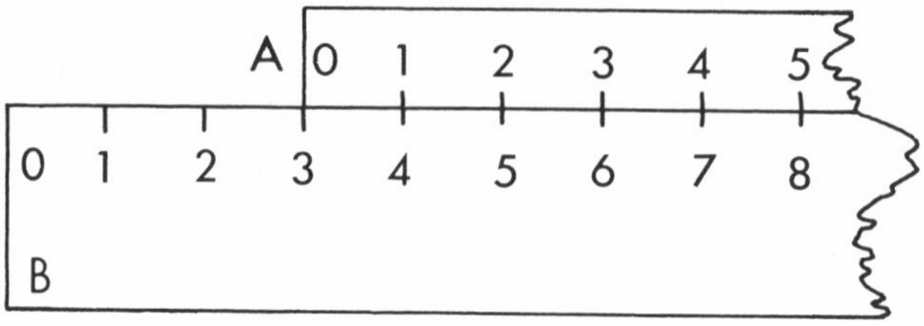

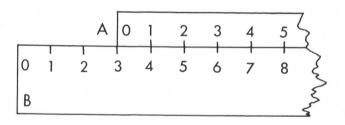

2. THINK **3 + N = 5** YOUR ANSWER IS DIRECTLY ABOVE **5** ON SLIDE **A.**

A
0 1 2 3 4 5
0 1 2 3 4 5 6 7 8
B

TRY THESE PROBLEMS ON THE **ADD—SUB** SLIDE RULE.

12 − 7 = N
8 − 2 = N
4 − 1 = N
11 − 8 = N

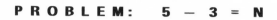

MORE CHALLENGING ADD-SUB SLIDE RULES ARE GIVEN ON THE NEXT PAGE IN THIS BOOK AND THE OTHER THREE AFTERMATH BOOKS.

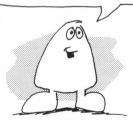

ADD-SUB SLIDE RULE

CUT OUT THIS **ADD-SUB** SLIDE RULE AND USE IT AS SHOWN ON THE PREVIOUS PAGES TO COMPLETE THE ADDITION TABLE BELOW.

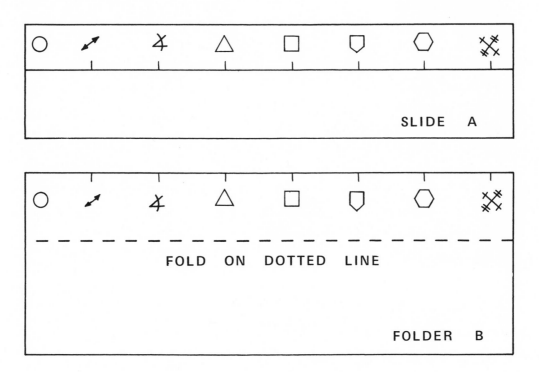

SLIDE A

FOLD ON DOTTED LINE

FOLDER B

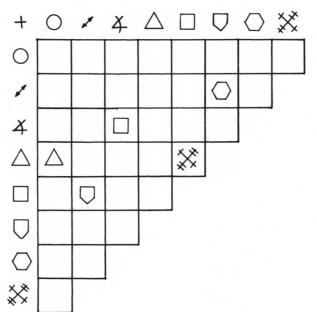

DO YOU KNOW WHY THIS AD-DITION TABLE IS NOT SQUARE?

19

FIFTEEN

I'M BORED.

KNOW ANY GOOD GAMES, DESI ?

SURE! A GOOD GAME FOR TWO IS "FIFTEEN."

WE START BY DRAWING A **TIC-TAC-TOE** DESIGN. ALSO WRITE DOWN THE NUMBERS 1 THROUGH 9.

1 2 3 4 5 6 7 8 9

YOU PLACE THE NUMBERS IN THE **TIC-TAC-TOE** SQUARES. THREE NUMBERS IN A LINE MUST ADD UP TO **FIFTEEN** OR YOU LOSE.

1 2 3 4 5 6 7 8 9

EXAMPLE:

6	4	5	= 15

LET'S PLAY.

1 2 3 4 5 6 7 8 9

OK! YOU START.

I CROSS OUT 4 UP HERE.

WHEN YOU USE A NUMBER, CROSS IT OUT. YOU CAN'T USE A NUMBER TWICE.

1 2 3 4 5 6 7 8 9

4

5

21

I USED 5 HERE, SO I HAVE TO CROSS IT OUT HERE.
6 UP HERE GIVES ME 15. DO I WIN?
NO! BUT IF YOU HAD PUT ANY OTHER NUMBER THERE, YOU WOULD HAVE LOST.

A PLAYER LOSES WHEN HE WRITES IN THE THIRD NUMBER IN A LINE THAT DOES **NOT** ADD UP TO 15.
I GOOFED.
THAT ADDS UP TO 16.

THIS IS A FUN GAME.
YOU HAVE TO USE ALL NINE NUMBERS. UNLESS YOU MAKE A "MAGIC SQUARE", SOMEBODY ALWAYS WINS.

TOWERS OF POWERS

COUNT THE SQUARES IN EACH REGION OF THE TOWER
AND WRITE AS THE POWER OF THE SAME NUMBER.

EXAMPLE:

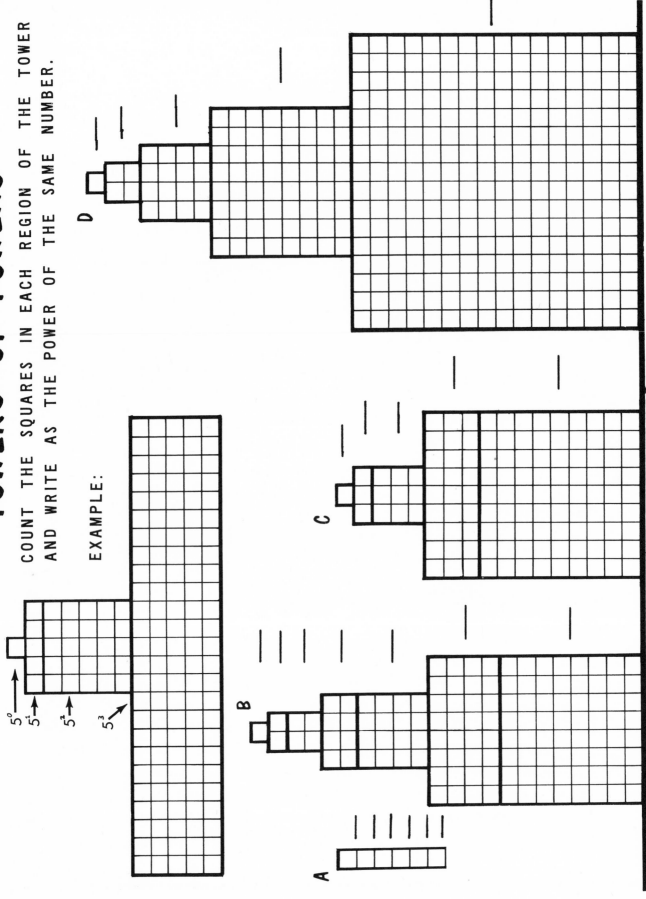

5^0
5^1
5^2
5^3

A

B

C

D

STAR SEARCH

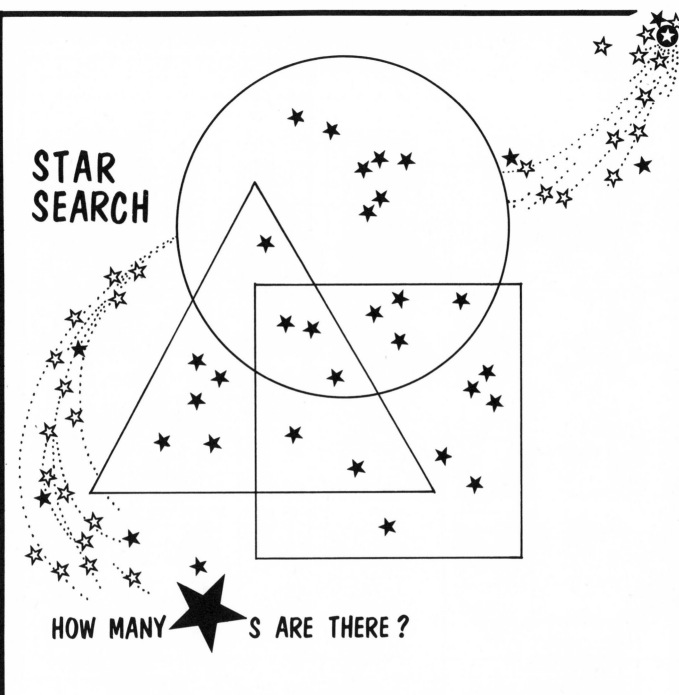

HOW MANY ⭐ S ARE THERE ?

_____ 1) IN THE CIRCLE, BUT NOT IN THE SQUARE OR TRIANGLE?
_____ 2) IN THE SQUARE, BUT NOT IN THE TRIANGLE OR CIRCLE?
_____ 3) COMMON TO THE TRIANGLE AND CIRCLE, BUT NOT THE SQUARE?
_____ 4) COMMON TO THE SQUARE AND CIRCLE, BUT NOT THE TRIANGLE?
_____ 5) IN THE TRIANGLE, BUT NOT IN THE SQUARE OR CIRCLE?
_____ 6) COMMON TO THE TRIANGLE AND SQUARE, BUT NOT THE CIRCLE?
_____ 7) COMMON TO THE CIRCLE, SQUARE AND TRIANGLE?

HIDDEN DESIGNS

THE EIGHT SHADED DESIGNS BELOW ARE ALL CREATED FROM THE PATTERN IN THE CENTER. CAN YOU SEE HOW EACH DESIGN WAS MADE? PLACE A PIECE OF TRACING PAPER OVER THE CENTER DESIGN AND MAKE SOME DESIGNS OF YOUR OWN.

PUZZLERS

FIVE BOYS RAN A 440 YARD DASH. A CAME IN FIRST.
B CAME IN LAST. IF D WAS AHEAD OF C, AND E WAS
JUST BEHIND HIM, WHO CAME IN SECOND?

THE YEAR 1936 WAS A SQUARE YEAR.
WHAT IS THE NEXT YEAR THAT WILL
BE SQUARE?

WAS IT A SQUARE YEAR, OR A YEAR FOR SQUARES?

1936

WRITE ELEVEN THOUSAND
ELEVEN HUNDRED, ELEVEN.

CAREFUL!

CAN YOU ARRANGE THESE
GLASSES, ALTERNATING
EMPTY AND FULL, BY
MOVING ONLY ONE OF
THEM?

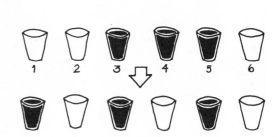

DOT-DOT-DOT···

HOW LONG WOULD IT TAKE YOU TO WRITE THE FIRST **MILLION** COUNTING NUMBERS?

OH, ABOUT **30 SECONDS.**

THAT'S RIDICULOUS. IT WOULD TAKE **MONTHS!**

OH YEAH? LET ME SHOW YOU.

HEY! THAT'S NOT FAIR! WHAT ARE THOSE DOTS?

1, 2, 3, 4, 5, 6, ••• 999,999, 1,000,000

THE SYMBOL ••• MEANS "CONTINUING IN THE SAME PATTERN." WHEN YOU ARE WRITING A LONG SEQUENCE OR SERIES OF NUMBERS, IT IS NICE TO USE THIS SEQUENCE.

IT MEANS "AD INFINITUM"!

OR, **AND SO ON!** • • •

WRITE THE FIRST:

1. HUNDRED COUNTING NUMBERS.
2. EIGHTY WHOLE NUMBERS.
3. HUNDRED EVEN NUMBERS.
4. FORTY ODD NUMBERS.

THIS PUZZLE LOOKS LIKE IT WAS MADE FROM TINKERTOYS.

THE THREE NUMBERS IN A LINE SHOULD ADD UP TO THE SAME NUMBER.

HERE'S AN EXAMPLE OF A COMPLETED TINKERTOTAL.

ANY WAY YOU GO, IT ADDS UP TO NINE!

AMAZING!

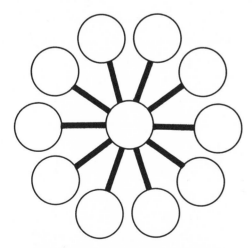

CAN YOU COMPLETE THESE TINKERTOTALS?

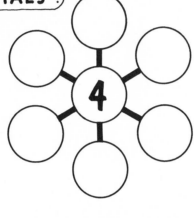

USE THE FIRST SEVEN COUNTING NUMBERS.

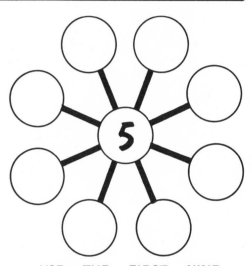

USE THE FIRST NINE COUNTING NUMBERS.

USE THE FIRST ELEVEN COUNTING NUMBERS.

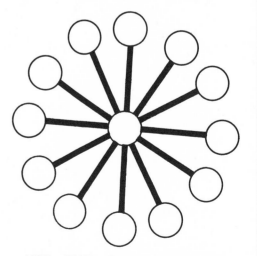

USE THE FIRST THIRTEEN COUNTING NUMBERS.

27

(CONTINUED)

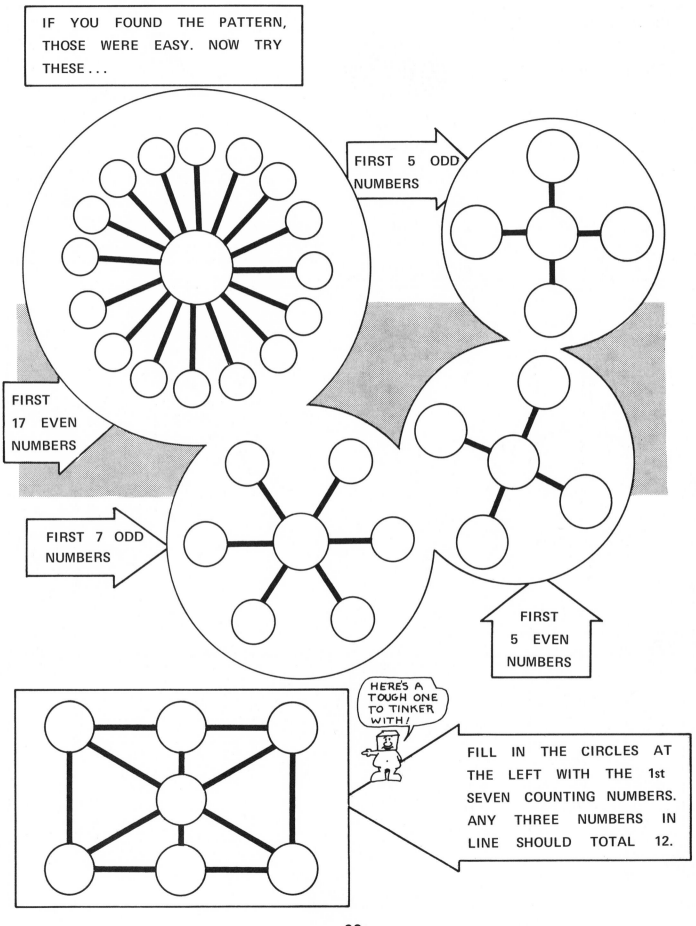

IF YOU FOUND THE PATTERN, THOSE WERE EASY. NOW TRY THESE . . .

FIRST 5 ODD NUMBERS

FIRST 17 EVEN NUMBERS

FIRST 7 ODD NUMBERS

FIRST 5 EVEN NUMBERS

HERE'S A TOUGH ONE TO TINKER WITH!

FILL IN THE CIRCLES AT THE LEFT WITH THE 1st SEVEN COUNTING NUMBERS. ANY THREE NUMBERS IN LINE SHOULD TOTAL 12.

WHIRLING WHEELS

MOVE THIS PAGE IN A CIRCULAR MOTION AND WATCH THE WHEELS WHIRL.

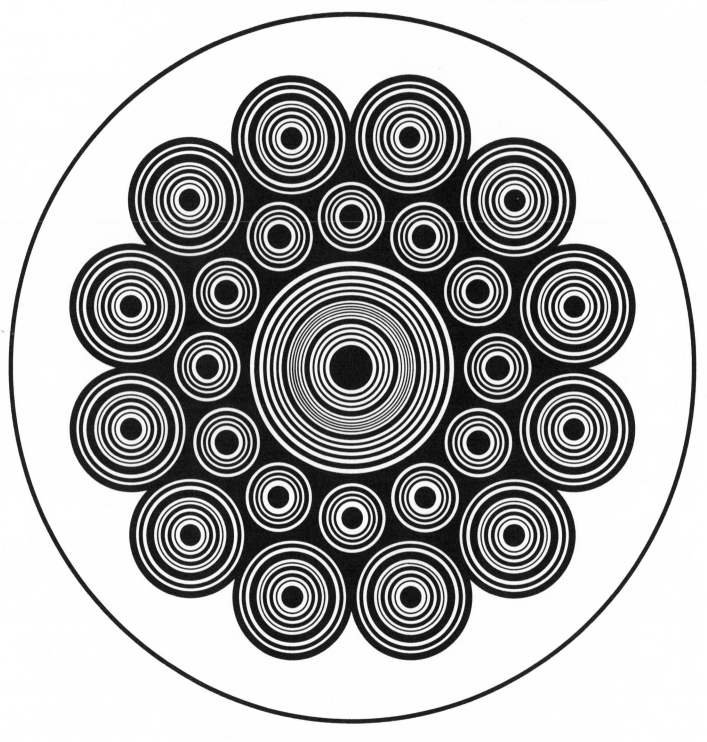

TILE TRIAL

USING ANY **THREE** OF THESE TILES, CAN YOU COMPLETE THE FOLLOWING SENTENCES?

HERE'S AN **EXAMPLE:**

$6 + 3 + 2 = 11$

5

$\square - \square + \square = 5$

1

$\square - \square - \square = 0$

6

$\square + \square - \square = 7$

2

$\square + \square - \square = 1$

7

$\square + \square - \square = 8$

3

$\square + \square - \square = 3$

8

$\square + \square + \square = 9$

4

$\square + \square - \square = 4$

HOW MANY DIFFERENT ANSWERS COULD YOU GET IF YOU USED ALL **FOUR** TILES?

31

32

HE SAID, "IF I HAVE SEEN A LITTLE FARTHER THAN OTHERS, IT IS BECAUSE I HAVE STOOD ON THE SHOULDERS OF GIANTS".

AS A __(1)__ EW BORN BABY, ON CHRISTMAS DAY, 1642, HE WAS "TINY ENOUGH TO FIT IN A QUART MUG."

HE EXPLAINED WHY THE SUN, MOON, AND STARS MOVE ON __(2)__ LLIPTIC PATHS.

HE CONSIDERED GEOMETRICAL QUANTITIES AS FORMED BY CONTINUOUS MOTION. THUS, A MOVING POINT FORMS A LINE. __(3)__ HAT DOES A MOVING LINE FORM?

HE HELPED MAN INTERPRET THE FALL OF AN APPLE FROM A __(4)__ REE.

HE DISCOVERED HOW A PRISM BREAKS UP LIGHT, AND MADE A SMALL REFLECTING TELESCOPE WHICH GAVE HIM A CLEAR IMAGE __(5)__ F THE STARS.

HE CALCULATED THE TOTAL AREA UNDER A CURVE BY ADDING THE AREA OF MANY SMALL RECTANGLES. HE I __(6)__ VENTED SOME OF THE CALCULUS.

___ ___ ___ ___ ___ ___
 1   2   3   4   5   6

1642-1727

SHAPES QUIZ

CAN YOU IDENTIFY
EACH OF THE
SHAPES BELOW?

RECTANGLE   PENTAGRAM   TRIANGLE   RHOMBUS   TRAPEZOID   ARC   SEMICIRCLE   ELLIPSE   SQUARE   PARALLELOGRAM   CIRCLE   ANGLE

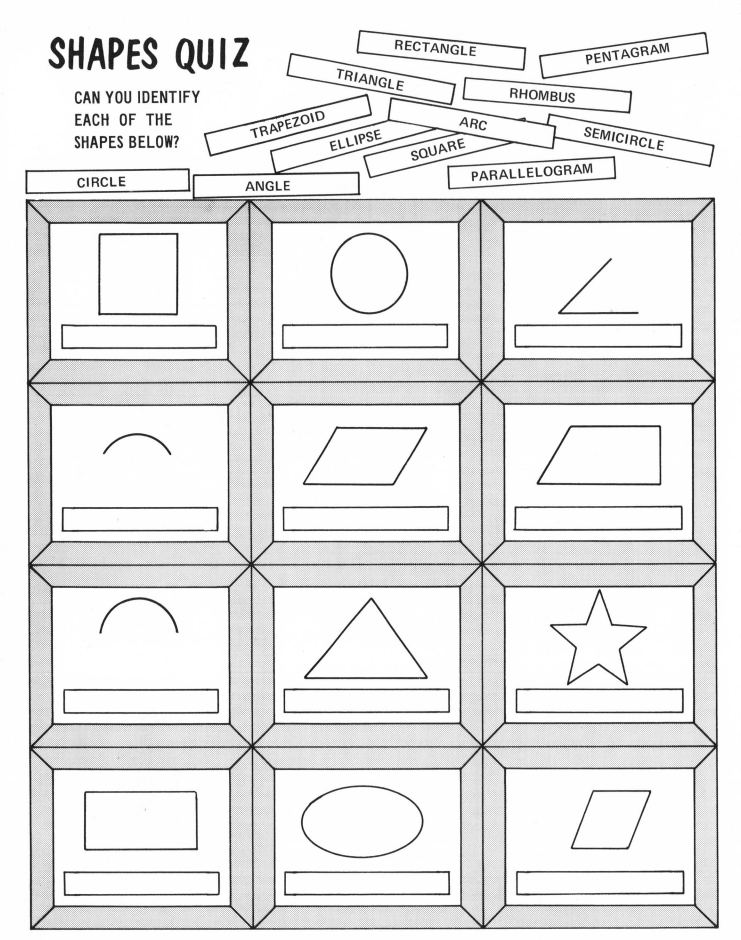

34

HOW MANY SQUARE UNITS DOES THIS TRIANGLE CONTAIN?

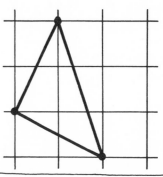

THE STEPS BELOW SHOW ONE WAY TO SOLVE THIS PROBLEM.

1 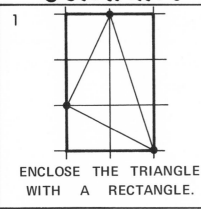 ENCLOSE THE TRIANGLE WITH A RECTANGLE.	2 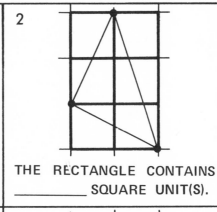 THE RECTANGLE CONTAINS _____ SQUARE UNIT(S).	3 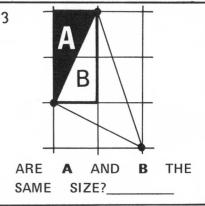 ARE **A** AND **B** THE SAME SIZE?_____
4 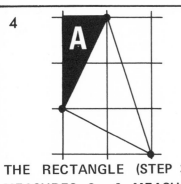 THE RECTANGLE (STEP 3) MEASURES 2. **A** MEASURES _____ SQUARE UNIT(S).	5 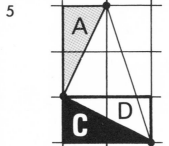 ARE **C** AND **D** THE SAME SIZE?_____	6 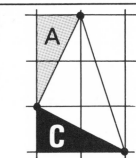 **C** MEASURES _____ SQUARE UNIT(S).
7 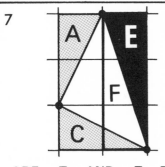 ARE **E** AND **F** THE SAME SIZE?_____	8 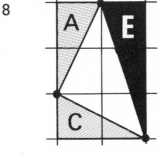 **E** COVERS ONE-HALF OF THREE SQUARES OR _____ SQUARES.	9 SUBTRACT **A**, **C**, AND **E** FROM THE RECTANGLE TO FIND THE MEASURE OF **G**. **G** WOULD COVER_____ SQUARES.

35

FIND THE NUMBER
OF **SQUARE UNITS**
EACH TRIANGLE
CONTAINS.

USE THE METHOD
SHOWN ON THE
PREVIOUS PAGE.

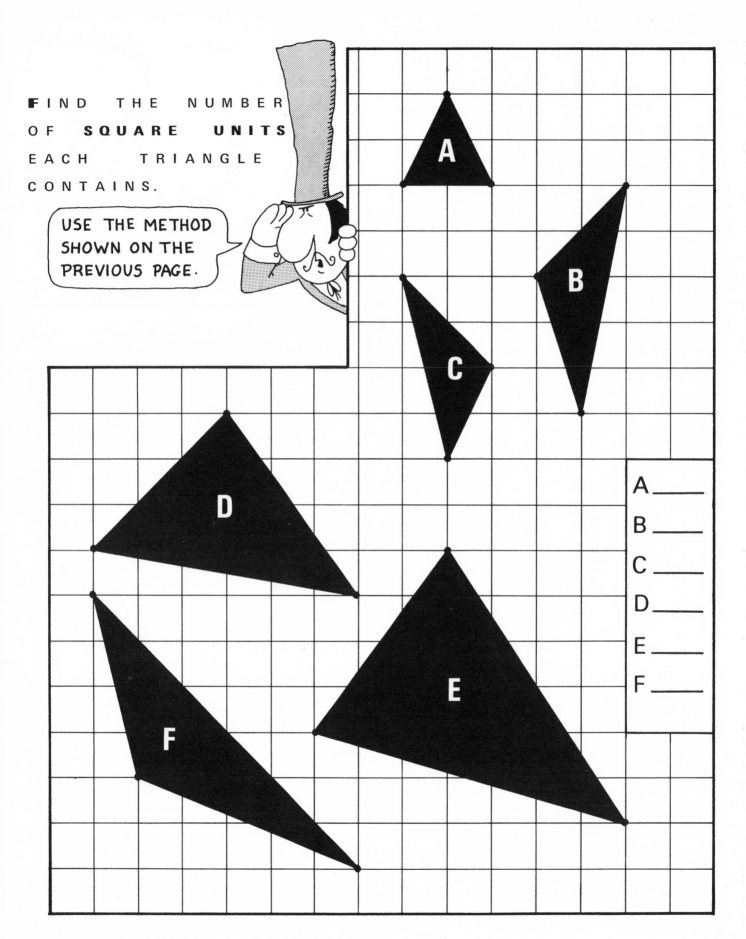

A____
B____
C____
D____
E____
F____

LINE DESIGN

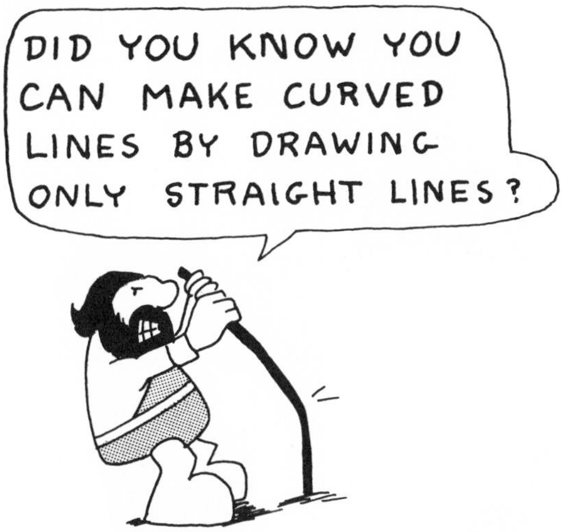

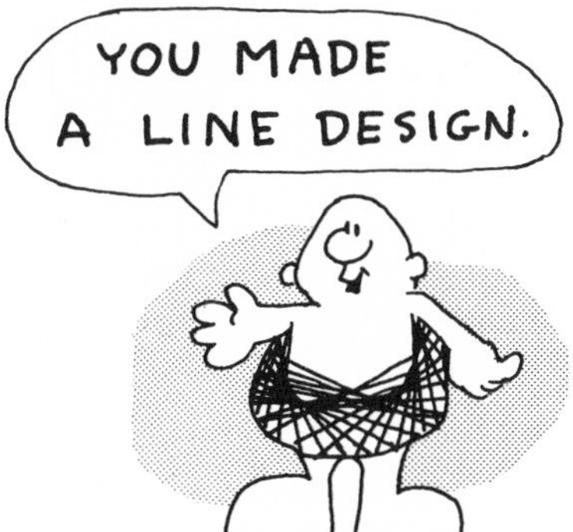

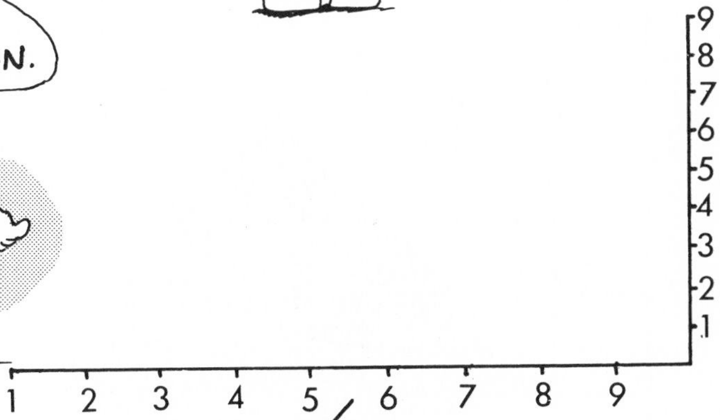

DID YOU KNOW YOU CAN MAKE CURVED LINES BY DRAWING ONLY STRAIGHT LINES?

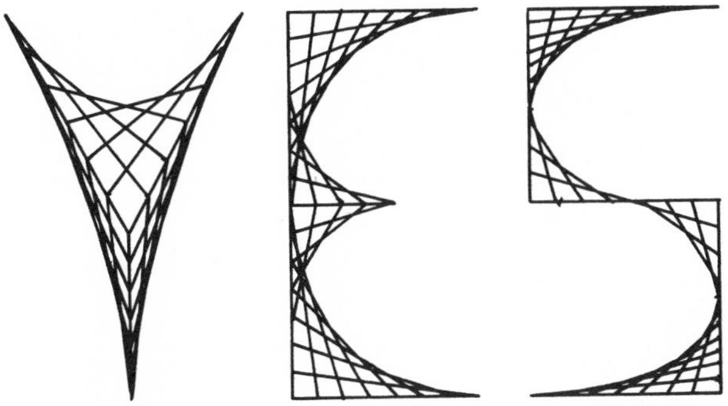

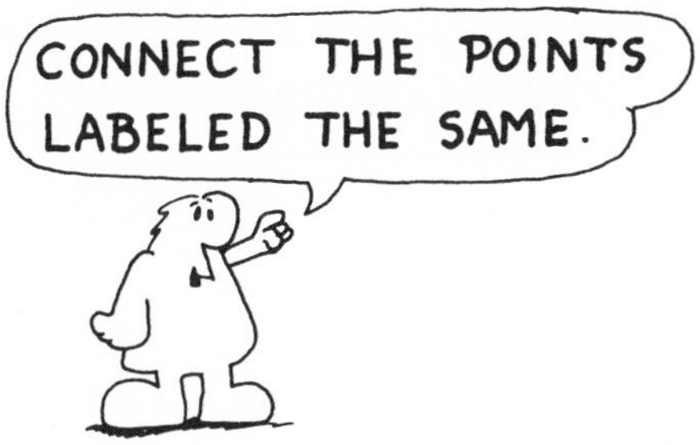

YES

CONNECT THE POINTS LABELED THE SAME.

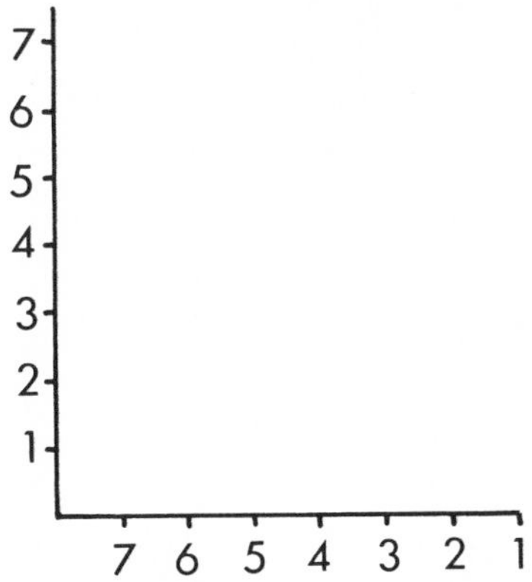

YOU MADE A LINE DESIGN.

TRY TWO ANGLES.

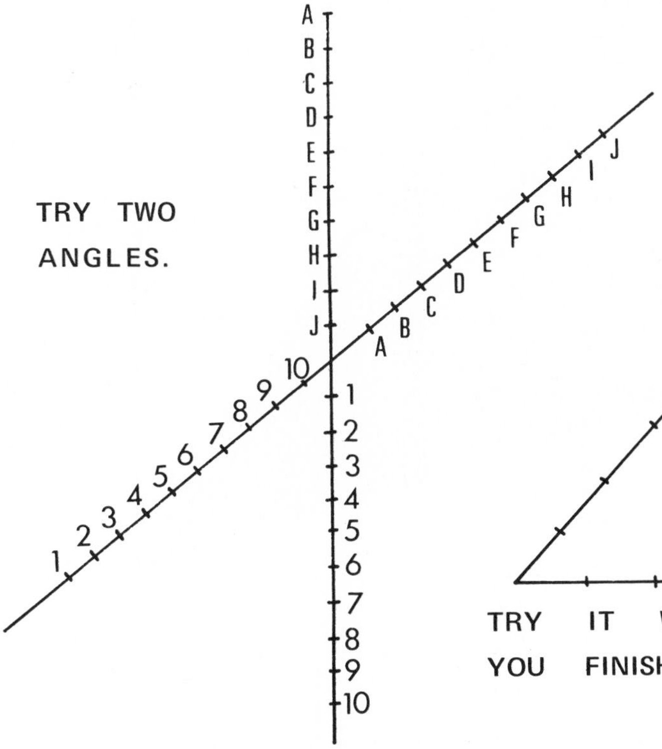

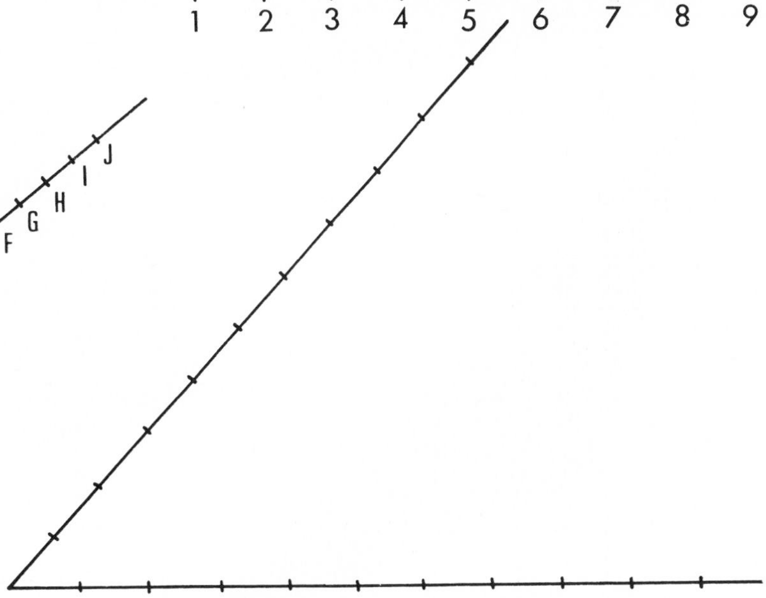

TRY IT WITHOUT THE NUMBERS. WHEN YOU FINISH, SHADE LIKE A CHECKERBOARD.

37

DIVISIBILITY

A NUMBER IS **DIVISIBLE** BY **TWO** IF ITS ONES DIGIT IS 0, 2, 4, 6 OR 8.

CIRCLE THE NUMBERS DIVISIBLE BY TWO.

162 24986 4560 295283 1331 2009 82588 39604 789315 57

DIVISIBLE BY TWO MEANS WHEN YOU DIVIDE BY TWO THERE IS NO REMAINDER.

```
      2359
   2 /4718
      4
      7
      6
      11
      10
      18
      18
```

ALL EVEN NUMBERS ARE DIVISIBLE BY TWO.

0 2 4 6 8

EVEN I KNEW THAT!

VERY PUNNY!

WHICH NUMBERS BELOW DOES TWO DIVIDE EVENLY?

YES   NO

_____ _____ A) 6, 789

_____ _____ B) 67, 894

_____ _____ C) 678, 912

_____ _____ D) 23, 579, 468

_____ _____ E) 891, 234, 567

YES   NO

_____ _____ F) 2, 345, 123, 451, 234, 512, 345

_____ _____ G) 4, 512, 345, 123, 451, 234, 512

_____ _____ H) 3, 451, 234, 512, 345, 123, 451

_____ _____ I) 5, 123, 451, 234, 512, 345, 123

_____ _____ J) 1, 234, 512, 345, 123, 451, 234

(CONTINUED)

DIVISIBILITY

A NUMBER IS **DIVISIBLE** BY **THREE** IF THE SUM OF ITS DIGITS IS DIVISIBLE BY THREE

WHAT'S A **DIGIT**, CAROL?

THERE ARE **TEN** DIGITS... 0 1 2 3 4 5 6 7 8 AND 9.

YOU MEAN 10 ISN'T A DIGIT?

NO, TEN IS MADE FROM **TWO** DIGITS, 1 AND 0.

FIND THE SUM OF THE DIGITS.

A. $46 \rightarrow 4+6 = $ _____

B. $123 \rightarrow 1+2+3 = $ _____

C. $57 \rightarrow 5+7 = $ _____

D. $495 \rightarrow 4+9+5 = $ _____

E. $2364 \rightarrow 2+3+6+4 = $ _____

F. $798032 \rightarrow 7+9+8+0+3+2 = $ _____

57 IS DIVISIBLE BY THREE SINCE **5 + 7 = 12** AND THREE DIVIDES 12 EVENLY.

$$\begin{array}{r} 19 \\ 3\overline{)57} \\ \underline{3} \\ 27 \\ \underline{27} \end{array}$$

$$\begin{array}{r} 4 \\ 3\overline{)12} \\ \underline{12} \end{array}$$

WHICH NUMBERS ARE DIVISIBLE BY **THREE**? (CIRCLE)

A. 51   B. 52   C. 63

D. 67   E. 333   F. 313

G. 818181   H. 76543

I. 1001001

40

(CONTINUED)

DIVISIBILITY

A NUMBER IS **DIVISIBLE** BY **FOUR** IF ITS LAST TWO DIGITS ARE DIVISIBLE BY FOUR.

FOR EXAMPLE: 39786520 IS DIVISIBLE BY FOUR.

3978652**0**

$$\begin{array}{r} 5 \\ 4\overline{)20} \\ 20 \end{array}$$

20 IS DIVISIBLE BY FOUR

WHICH NUMBERS ARE DIVISIBLE BY FOUR?

A   349,607,153,246,844
B   76,529,137,880,265,743
C   9,001,200,573,642,850
D   444,445,555,666,676
E   898,053,211,524,600

IT'S UPSIDE DOWN, DUMMY!

A NUMBER IS DIVISIBLE BY FIVE IF IT ENDS IN **0** OR **FIVE**.

CIRCLE THE NUMBERS THAT FIVE DIVIDES EVENLY.

11768   8326445920

500005

1989

26040

35

60606

4382917

7788992   895

630

27

3745   19263054

(CONTINUED)

DIVISIBILITY

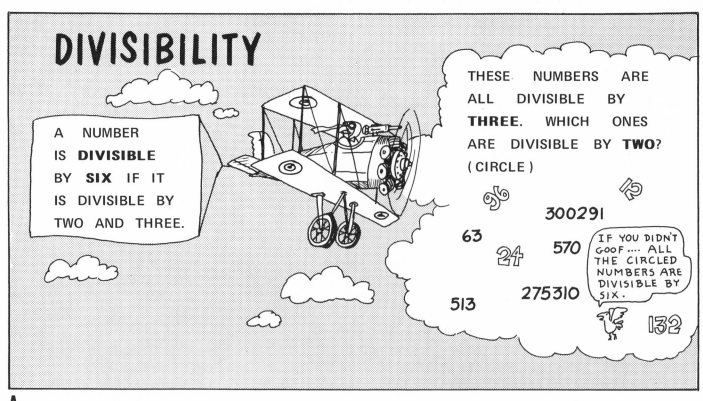

A NUMBER IS **DIVISIBLE** BY **SIX** IF IT IS DIVISIBLE BY TWO AND THREE.

THESE NUMBERS ARE ALL DIVISIBLE BY **THREE**. WHICH ONES ARE DIVISIBLE BY **TWO**? (CIRCLE)

96   12
300291
63   570   IF YOU DIDN'T GOOF.... ALL THE CIRCLED NUMBERS ARE DIVISIBLE BY SIX.
24
513   275310   132

A.

THESE NUMBERS ARE ALL DIVISIBLE BY **TWO**. WHICH ONES ARE DIVISIBLE BY **THREE**? (CIRCLE)

26   48   28

392

6254307891 73554

10   23610

4506   52876

84   100

ALL CIRCLED NUMBERS SHOULD BE DIVISIBLE BY SIX.

B. A NUMBER DIVISIBLE BY **SIX** IS DIVISIBLE BY

_____ AND _____.

C. CIRCLE THE NUMBERS BELOW THAT ARE DIVISIBLE BY **SIX**.

2570   3429

8372   5144

54   96   880

412   683

9025

42

MATH GOLF

THE NINE HOLES OF A MATH GOLF COURSE ARE **210,** **240,** **180,** **120,** **360,** **330,** **300,** **270** AND **420** YARDS IN LENGTH. A MATHE—MATICIAN PLAYING THIS COURSE ALWAYS STRIKES THE BALL IN A PERFECTLY STRAIGHT LINE AND SENDS IT EXACTLY ONE OF THREE DISTANCES. IT ALWAYS GOES STRAIGHT TOWARDS THE HOLE, PASSES OVER THE HOLE OR DROPS IN THE CUP. IF HE ALWAYS HITS THE BALL **60,** **90** OR **150** YARDS, WHAT IS THE LOWEST SCORE HE COULD HAVE ON NINE HOLES TO COMPLETE HIS SCORE CARD.

DIGIT COUNTRY CLUB SCORE CARD		
HOLE	YARDS	SCORE
1	210	
2	240	
3	180	
4	120	
5	360	
6	330	
7	300	
8	270	
9	420	
	TOTALS	

BIFF PUT TOGETHER A 3 X 3 X 3 CUBE.

THEN HE PAINTED THE SIX OUTSIDE FACES.

IF BIFF SEPARATED THE BLOCK INTO 27 CUBES...

HOW MANY SMALL CUBES WOULD HAVE...

3 FACES PAINTED? _____

2 FACES PAINTED? _____

1 FACE PAINTED? _____

0 FACES PAINTED? _____

CAN ANYONE IN YOUR BLOCK ANSWER THESE QUESTIONS?

TYPICAL BLOCKHEADED REMARK!

HOW MANY?

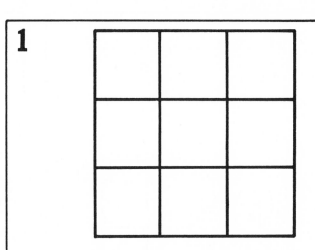

1

HOW MANY SQUARES IN THIS FIGURE? _____

2

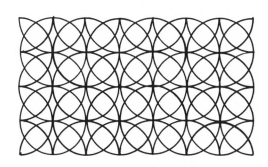

HOW MANY COMPLETE CIRCLES?

_____

3

HOW MANY LINE SEGMENTS CAN BE DRAWN TO CONNECT THE FOUR DOTS ABOVE? _____

4

HOW MANY WAYS CAN THE LETTERS

A,B,C AND D

BE WRITTEN...FOUR AT A TIME?

ABCD
ABDC

HERE ARE TWO!

~~AABC~~   DON'T USE A LETTER TWICE.

CAN YOU FIND **RULES** FOR PROBLEMS 1, 3 AND 4?

LOOK FOR PATTERNS.

45

REFER TO HATS ON PAGE 46.

A.

TWO OF THE HATS ARE CHECKED AND HAVE BANDS.

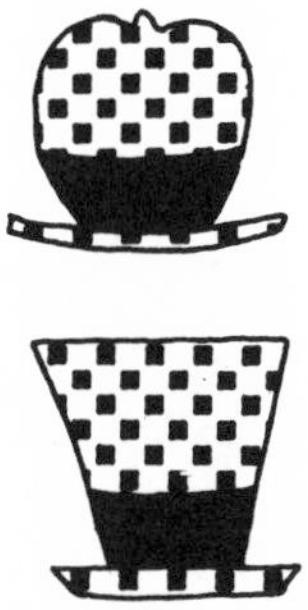

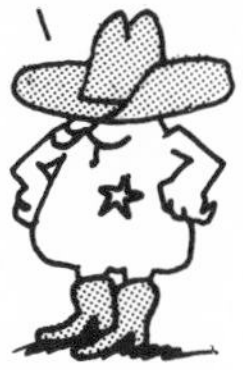

B.

HOW MANY HATS HAVE BANDS?

C.

HOW MANY CHECKED HATS HAVE BANDS BUT NO FEATHERS?

D.

3
16

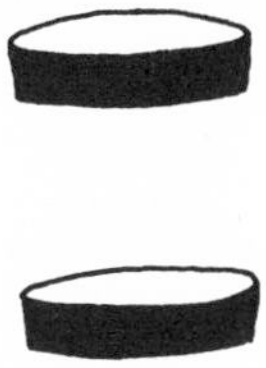

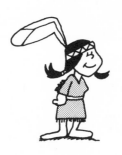

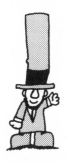

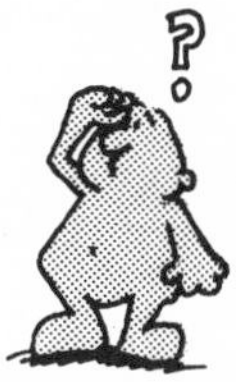

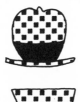

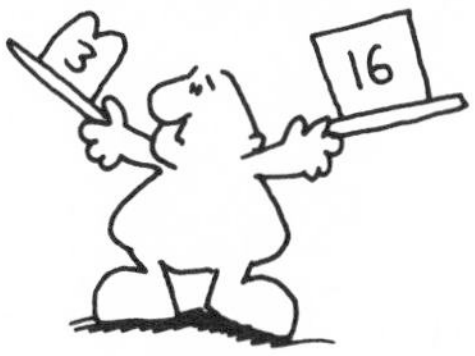

HAT # 3 AND # 16 HAVE WHAT COMMON ATTRIBUTE?

E.

WHICH TWO HATS ON THE SECOND SHELF HAVE THE SAME SHAPE?

F.

HOW MANY HATS HAVE BOTH BANDS AND FEATHERS?

G.

WHICH HATS HAVE THE SAME SHAPE AS HAT 18 ?

H.

HELP!

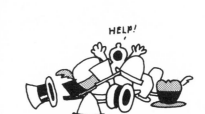

HAT # 5, 11 AND 15 HAVE WHAT COMMON ATTRIBUTE?

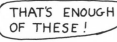

THAT'S ENOUGH OF THESE!
YEAH! I'VE HAT IT TOO!

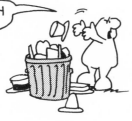

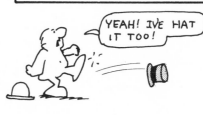

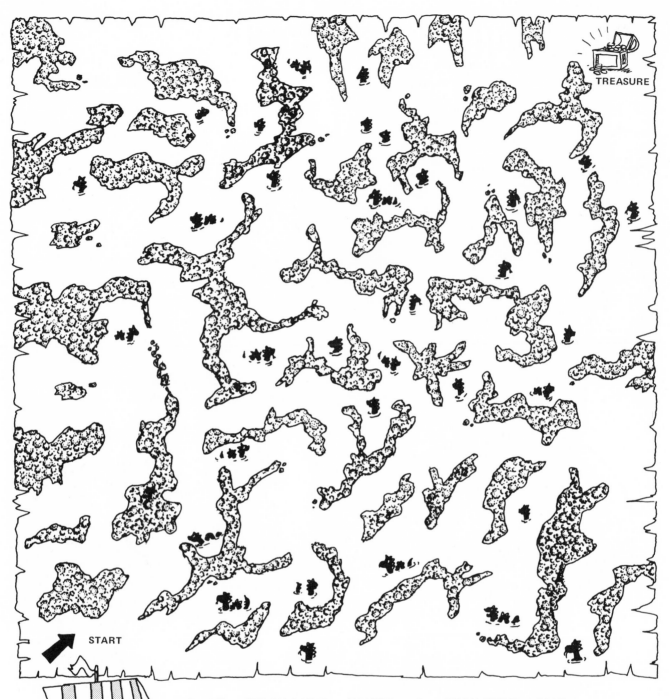

TREASURE

START

OLAF STRONGARM FOUND A TREASURE MAP. TO REACH THE TREASURE, OLAF HAD TO SAIL THROUGH A MAZE OF ISLANDS, WHICH IN ITSELF WAS NOT DIFFICULT, BUT THE WATERS NEAR THE ISLANDS WERE INFESTED WITH FIERCE SEA SERPENTS. OLAF FOUGHT THE SERPENTS OFF WITH SPEARS, BUT ONLY HAD ENOUGH SPEARS FOR TWO SERPENTS. HOW DID OLAF DO 'T?

CONSTRUCTING DESIGNS

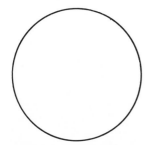

USE A COMPASS TO DRAW A CIRCLE.

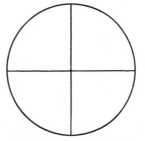

DIVIDE THE CIRCLE INTO FOUR CONGRU-ENT SECTIONS BY CONSTRUCTING TWO PERPENDICULAR DIAMETERS.

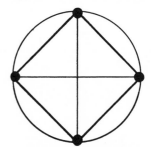

INSCRIBED SQUARE

CONNECT THE END-POINTS OF THE DIAMETERS TO INSCRIBE A SQUARE.

THE DESIGNS BELOW ARE BASED ON A SQUARE INSCRIBED IN A CIRCLE. CAN YOU CONSTRUCT THESE AND CREATE YOUR OWN?

49

MULTIPLE MADNESS

ISLAND **X** HAS A
POPULATION OF
1,000 PEOPLE.

EVERY 30 YEARS THE
POPULATION OF ISLAND **X**
DOUBLES.

FILL IN THE CHART.

POPULATION NOW	1,000
IN 30 YEARS	
IN 60 YEARS	
IN 90 YEARS	
IN 120 YEARS	
IN 150 YEARS	
IN 180 YEARS	
IN 210 YEARS	
IN 240 YEARS	
IN 270 YEARS	
IN 300 YEARS	

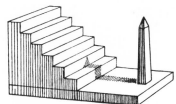

Egyptian temple steps
circa 2000 B.C.

Egyptian time piece
circa 1920 A.D.

CLOCK TALK

Even tempered dial *1341*

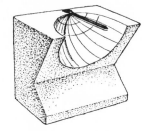

Greek sundial

HERE ARE SOME ANCIENT DEVICES FOR TELLING TIME. CAN YOU CREATE A SUN DIAL?

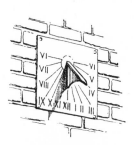

Wall dial

Saxon dial

Station clock

Dutch dial

Pocket dial

Summer   *Winter*

Japanese clock

Shepherd's clock

51

REASON TEASIN'

THIS KIND OF PUZZLE IS SOMETIMES CALLED A **LOGIC TEST**.

WANT TO LEARN HOW TO THINK **LOGICALLY**?

TRY THIS! HOW DO FIGURES **A + B** COMPARE?

A   B

THEY ARE THE SAME SHAPE, BUT **B** IS BIGGER.

THAT'S LOGIC?

WHAT KIND OF FIGURE COMPARES TO **C** LIKE **B** COMPARES TO **A**?

A BIGGER CIRCLE?

YES! NOW WE CAN WRITE:

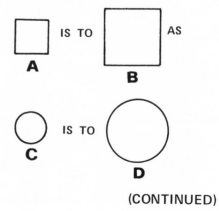

A IS TO B AS

C IS TO D

(CONTINUED)

IN THIS EXAMPLE, NUMBER FIVE IS THE CORRECT ANSWER. **B** CHANGES BY SHADING, SO **C** CHANGES BY SHADING ALSO.

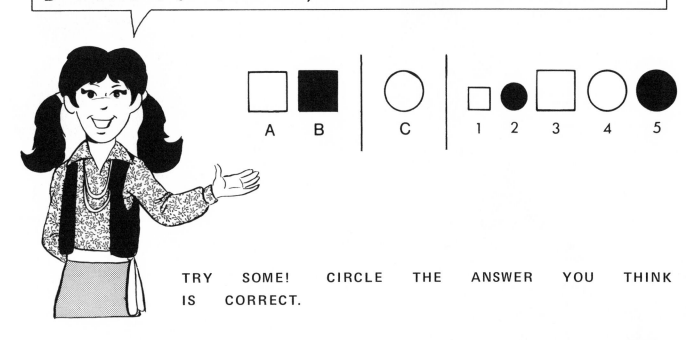

TRY SOME! CIRCLE THE ANSWER YOU THINK IS CORRECT.

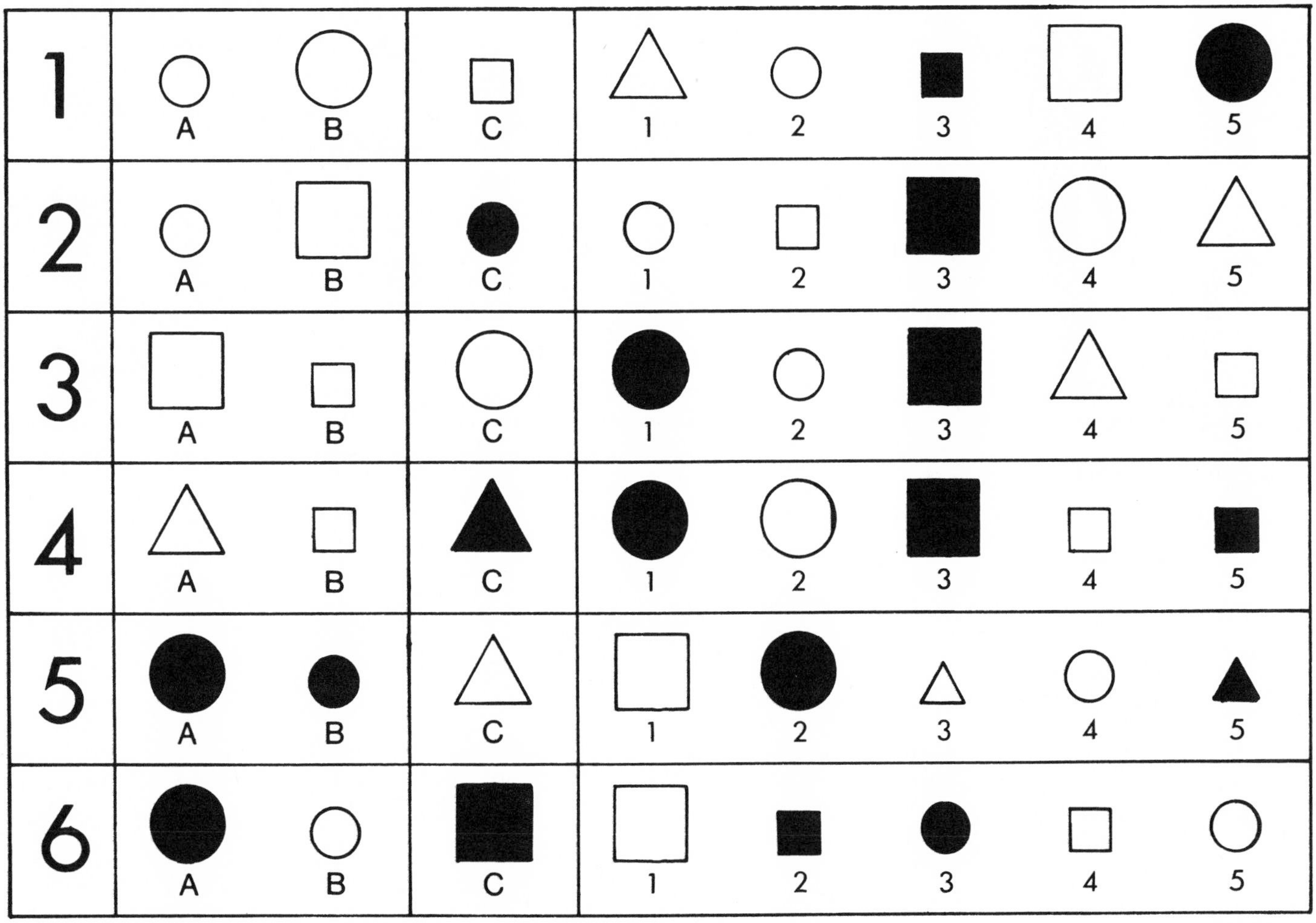

(CONTINUED)

53

REASON TEASIN'

IN THESE LOGIC PUZZLES, FIGURE **A** CHANGES TO **B** LIKE **C** CHANGES TO WHAT NUMBER?

THERE ARE MORE OF THESE IN BOOKS 2, 3, AND 4.

	A	B	C	1	2	3	4	5
1								
2								
3								
4								
5								
6								
7								

HEX NUMBER PUZZLE

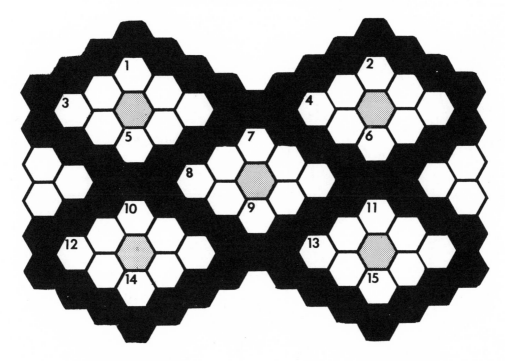

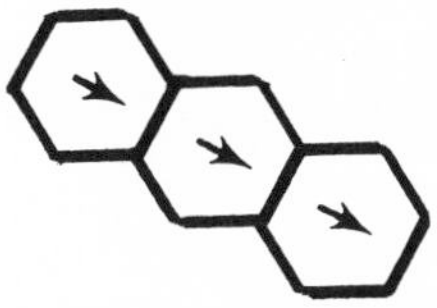

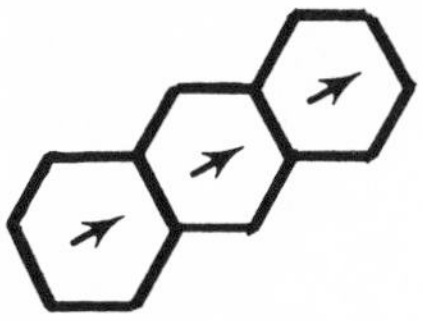

1. 27 x 13

2. 107 + 255

3. 858 – 439

4. 735 ÷ 7

7. 374 + 258

8. 3 x 219

10. 901 – 702

11. 963 ÷ 3

12. (45 + 172) + 201

13. 5 x (13 x 9)

3. 957 – 484

4. 138 + 45

5. 4805 ÷ 5

6. 4 x 4 x 4 x 4 x 2

8. 6 x 3 x 37

9. 4000 – 3258

12. 137 + 80 + 254

13. 1046 – 523

14. 9229 ÷ 11

15. 17 x 33

(CONTINUED)

CAN YOU SEE THE PATTERNS IN THIS **ARROWMATH** USING THE CHART BELOW?

1 → → | 1 | 7 | 13 | OR **13**

4 → → | | | | OR ___

15 → ↑ OR **20**

WILLIAM TELL WOULD HAVE LIKED THIS MATH.

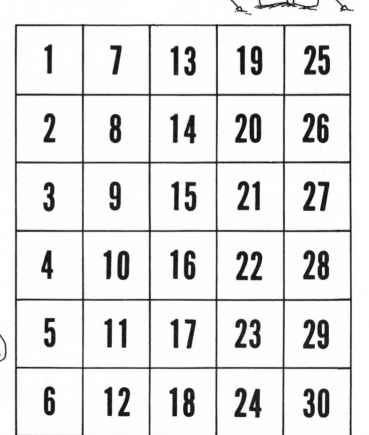

30 → | 30 | → WHOOPS! Ø OR { } NO ANSWER.

21 → ↓ ↑ | 21 | 27 |
          | | 28 | OR **27**

9 → ↓ ← ↑ | 9 | 15 |
            | 10 | 16 | OR **9**

THESE ARROWS REPRESENT **OPERATIONS** ON NUMBERS LIKE ADDITION AND SUBTRACTION.

1	7	13	19	25
2	8	14	20	26
3	9	15	21	27
4	10	16	22	28
5	11	17	23	29
6	12	18	24	30

CAN YOU SOLVE THESE **ARROWMATH** SENTENCES?

USE THE CHART ON THE PREVIOUS PAGE TO HELP YOU SOLVE THESE.

HOPE THEY DON'T SHOOT YOU DOWN!

A. 3 → → → _____

B. 17 ← ↑ → _____

C. HERE ARE SOME NEW **SYMBOLS.**

D. 10 → ↗ → ↘ _____

E. 14 ↘ ↙ ↖ ↗ _____

G. 23 ↑↑ ← ← ↓↓ → _____

H. 17 → ↓ ← ↑ ↗ ↘ _____

I. 26 ↓↓ ↗↗ ↑ ↖ _____

F. 22 ↑↑ ← ↗↓ → ↓↙↑ ↖↗ → ↙↘ → → ↑↑↑↗ _____

57

WHICH ONE DIFFERS ?

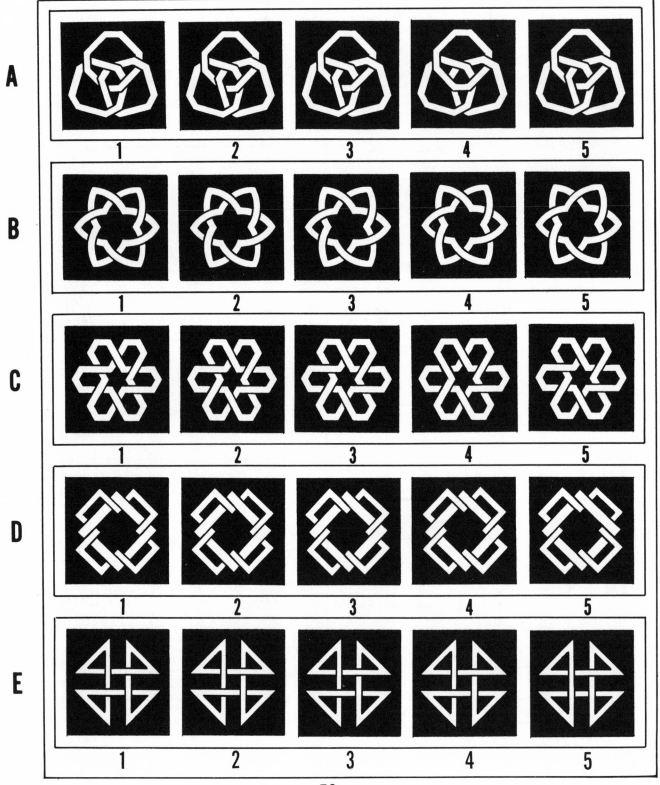

TRIANGLE THEOREM

DECODE THE MESSAGE

MOVING MATCHES

I. MAKE TWO TRIANGLES WITH FIVE MATCHES.

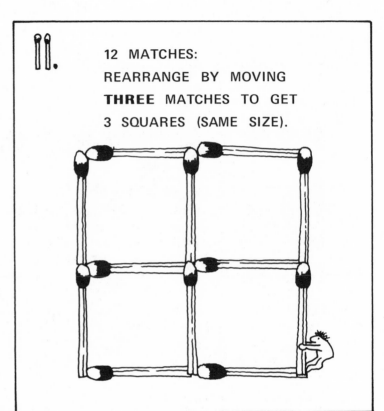

II. 12 MATCHES: REARRANGE BY MOVING **THREE** MATCHES TO GET 3 SQUARES (SAME SIZE).

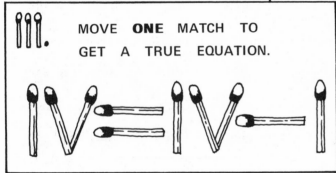

III. MOVE **ONE** MATCH TO GET A TRUE EQUATION.

IV = IV − I

CAREFUL HOW YOU USE THEM!

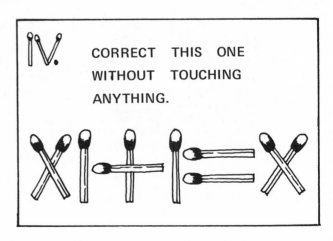

IV. CORRECT THIS ONE WITHOUT TOUCHING ANYTHING.

XI + I = X

60

PATTERNS AND SEQUENCES

FIND THE PATTERN AND FILL IN THE MISSING NUMBERS.

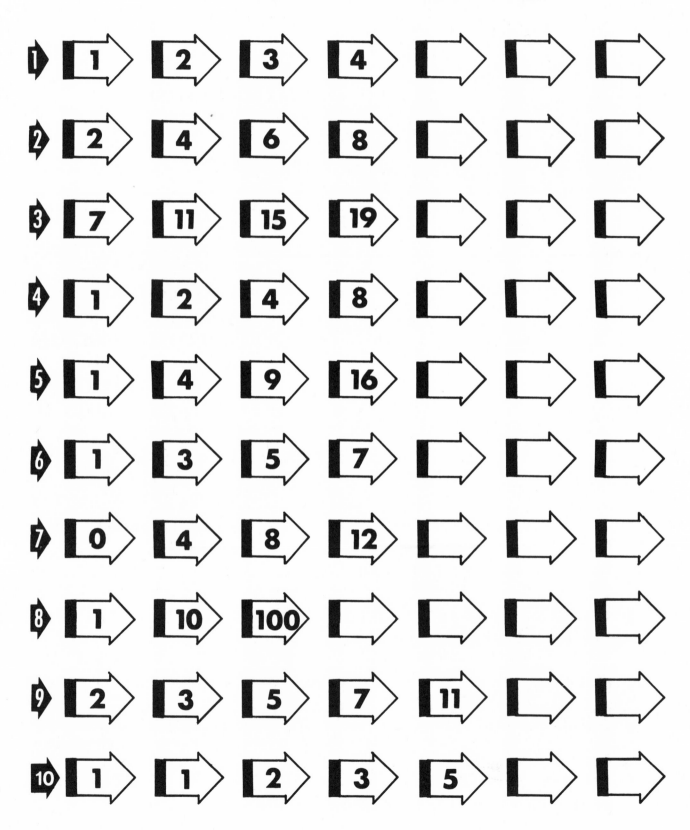

1) 1 2 3 4

2) 2 4 6 8

3) 7 11 15 19

4) 1 2 4 8

5) 1 4 9 16

6) 1 3 5 7

7) 0 4 8 12

8) 1 10 100

9) 2 3 5 7 11

10) 1 1 2 3 5

PEG PUZZLE PLANS

HERE ARE PLANS FOR A SOLITAIRE PEG PUZZLE GAME THAT YOU CAN MAKE YOURSELF.

MATERIALS NEEDED:

ONE PIECE OF WOOD 3/4" TO 1" THICK
ONE DOWEL STICK (3/16" OR 1/4")
   36" LONG
QUARTER-INCH DRILL
HANDSAW AND SANDPAPER

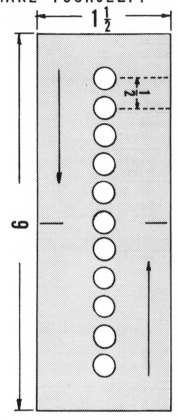

CONSTRUCTION:

1) CUT BOARD 1-1/2" X 6" OR LARGER, IF YOU PREFER.
2) MARK LOCATION OF HOLES TO BE DRILLED.
3) DRILL HOLES A UNIFORM DEPTH. A 3/16" OR 1/4" DRILL BIT IS PROBABLY THE BEST SIZE. DRILL SOME TEST HOLES IN SCRAP BOARD TO SEE HOW THE DOWEL STICK FITS IN THE HOLE.
4) CUT 10 PEGS FROM THE DOWEL STICK THE DESIRED LENGTH.
5) PAINT FIVE PEGS ONE COLOR AND THE OTHER FIVE, A SECOND COLOR.

RULES:

1) PLACE FIVE PEGS OF ONE COLOR AT ONE END OF THE BOARD AND FIVE PEGS OF THE SECOND COLOR AT THE OTHER END OF THE BOARD. THIS LEAVES THE CENTER HOLE OPEN.

2) OBJECT OF THE GAME IS TO MOVE EACH SET OF PEGS TO THE OPPOSITE END OF THE BOARD.

3) A PEG MAY BE MOVED BY MOVING ONE HOLE FORWARD OR BY JUMPING.

4) MOVING OR JUMPING BACKWARD IS NOT ALLOWED.

5) YOU HAVE WON THE GAME IF YOU FINISH WITH THE PEGS COMPLETELY REVERSED FROM THE STARTING POSITION.

MULTIPLE MAZE

MOVE FROM START TO
FINISH BY FOLLOWING
A PATH OF MULTIPLES.

START

7	14	20	27	54	61	76	83
13	21	27	44	55	63	70	77
20	28	35	42	49	56	90	84
27	34	41	48	55	62	97	91
160	153	146	139	132	125	104	98
154	147	140	133	126	119	112	105
161	167	188	195	202	227	216	111
168	175	182	189	196	203	210	217

FINISH

START

3	2	5	6	13	17	37	58	59	64
6	4	14	7	16	19	35	61	62	65
9	12	15	18	20	22	32	67	68	70
11	8	10	21	23	31	66	69	72	75
33	30	27	24	25	34	63	73	71	78
36	28	26	29	30	74	60	94	95	81
39	42	45	48	51	54	57	93	87	84
38	40	41	47	76	77	78	80	90	97
43	44	46	49	85	83	79	87	93	92
50	52	53	56	86	89	88	91	96	99

FINISH

DO NOT CONNECT
SQUARES WITH
A DIAGONAL.

START

9	17	26	71	107	162	171	180
18	28	53	62	161	153	188	189
27	36	45	55	152	144	197	198
26	44	54	62	143	135	206	207
35	71	63	73	125	126	215	216
89	80	72	82	109	117	125	225
98	91	81	90	99	108	118	234
107	100	89	98	107	116	127	243

FINISH

64

PRIME TIME

EVERY COMPOSITE NUMBER CAN BE FACTORED UNIQUELY INTO PRIME FACTORS.

TRANSLATED, THAT MEANS A NUMBER CAN BE BROKEN UP INTO PRIMES IN ONLY ONE WAY.

CIRCULAR REASONING

CAROL CASHEW, MILD—MANNERED SECRETARY FOR A GREAT METROPOLITAN PUBLISHING COMPANY (WHO IS, IN REALITY, "LIGHTFOOTED LADY", CHAMPION OF JUSTICE AND NEMESIS OF EVILDOERS) WAS ON HER WAY TO PUT OUT A FIRE SALE, WHEN SHE WAS CONFRONTED BY A MAZE BUILT BY HER ARCH ENEMY, THE EVIL "SUFFERING SMYTH". NOT HESITATING, SHE WEAVED HER WAY THROUGH THE MAZE AND ARRIVED AT THE FIRE SALE IN THE NICK OF TIME. HOW DID SHE DO IT?

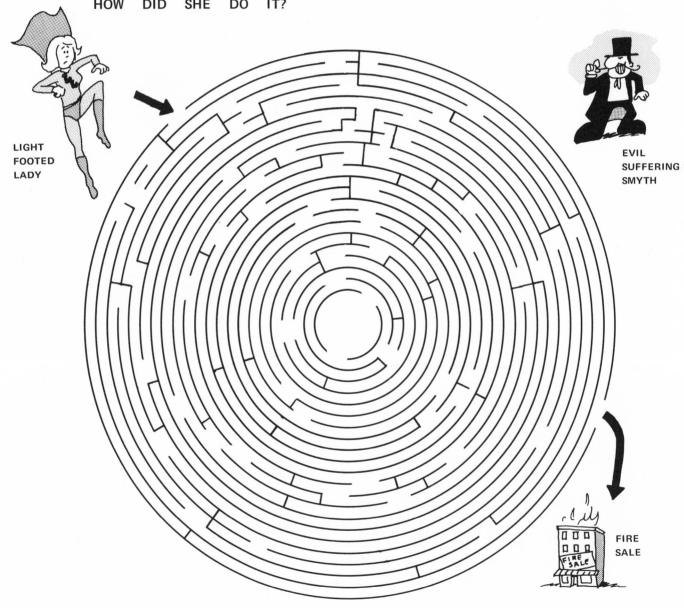

LIGHT
FOOTED
LADY

EVIL
SUFFERING
SMYTH

FIRE
SALE

AVERAGES

AN AVERAGE IS THE
SUM OF A SET OF
NUMBERS DIVIDED BY
THE NUMBER OF NUMBERS.

WHAT IS THEIR AVERAGE
HAT SIZE?

DAD – 7½

MOM – 6¾

BIG BROTHER
7½

LITTLE SISTER
6¾

JUNIOR – 6½

WHAT IS THE AVERAGE
AGE OF THIS FAMILY?

JUNIOR
4

MOM
39?

DAD
43

BIG BROTHER
15

LITTLE SISTER
9

73"   68"   71"   59"   39"

WHAT IS THE AVERAGE
HEIGHT OF THIS FAMILY?

TRELLIS TWISTER

THE TRELLIS IN THE TOP LEFT-HAND CORNER IS ONE OF THE OTHER EIGHT AS SEEN FROM THE BACK SIDE. WHICH ONE?

DIJAKNOWTHAT

A MILLION NICKELS PLACED IN ONE LINE WILL
STRETCH ABOUT 13 MILES?

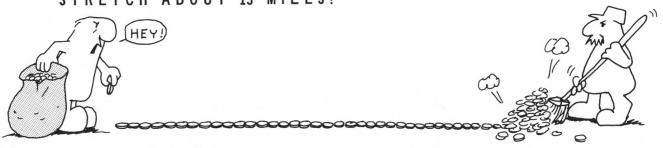

A BARREL FILLED WITH DIMES WOULD BE WORTH ABOUT
20% MORE THAN A BARREL FILLED WITH HALF DOLLARS?
(THERE WOULD BE ABOUT SIX TIMES AS MANY DIMES AS
HALF DOLLARS).

A ROUND CLOTH DRIES FASTER THAN A SQUARE CLOTH?
(THE CORNERS OF A SQUARE CLOTH HOLD THE MOISTURE
LONGER. CLOTH USUALLY DRIES FROM THE CENTER
OUTWARDS.)

$$999999 \cdot 2 = 1999998$$
$$999999 \cdot 3 = 2999997$$
$$999999 \cdot 4 = 3999996$$
$$999999 \cdot 5 = 4999995$$
$$999999 \cdot 6 = 5999994$$
$$999999 \cdot 7 = 6999993$$
$$999999 \cdot 8 = 7999992$$
$$999999 \cdot 9 = \underline{}$$

HELLO THERE! I'D LIKE YOU TO MEET SOME FRIENDS OF MINE. THEY MAY SEEM A LITTLE STRANGE AT FIRST, BUT THEY'RE PRETTY USEFUL ONCE YOU GET TO KNOW THEM.

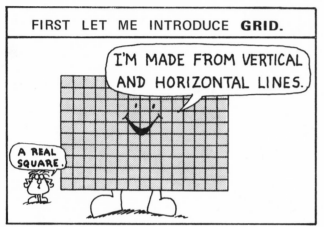

FIRST LET ME INTRODUCE **GRID**.

I'M MADE FROM VERTICAL AND HORIZONTAL LINES.

A REAL SQUARE.

NEXT, WE HAVE THE TWO AXIS BROTHERS, **VERTICAL** AND **HORIZONTAL**.

OUR FRIENDS CALL US "**V**" AND "**H**" FOR SHORT.

V E R T I C A L

HO _ _ _ _ _ _ _ _

THIS SLEEPY LOOKING FELLOW IS CALLED **ORDERED PAIR**. WHEN BOTH HIS EYES ARE OPEN YOU SEE A PAIR OF NUMBERS.

1 ,

I'M OFTEN SEEN WITH A POINT BECAUSE I **LOCATE** A POINT.

7 , 5

GET THE POINT

H, V, THE POINTS AND I SPEND MOST OF OUR TIME PLAYING ON THE **BIG GRID**.

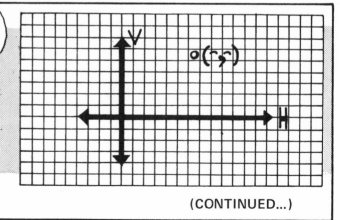

(CONTINUED...)

70

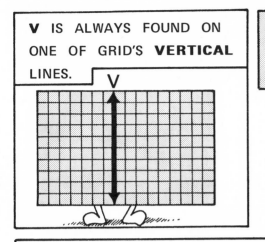

V IS ALWAYS FOUND ON ONE OF GRID'S **VERTICAL** LINES.

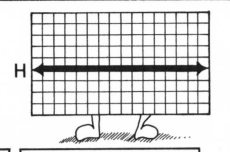

H IS ALWAYS FOUND ON ONE OF GRID'S **HORIZONTAL** LINES.

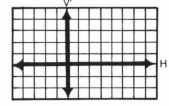

H AND **V** ARE USUALLY FOUND TOGETHER.

NOTICE H AND V ARE WIDER AND DARKER THAN GRID'S LINES.

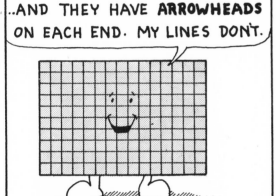

..AND THEY HAVE **ARROWHEADS** ON EACH END. MY LINES DON'T.

MY NAME IS NOT A WORD BUT A PAIR OF **NUMBERS**. MY NAME IS **FOUR, SIX**.

(4, 6)

DO YOU SPELL THAT 40UR, 6IX?

(—, 2) • MY NAME IS THREE, TWO.

(7, 1) • MY NAME IS SEVEN, ONE.

• WE NAME **POINTS**.

CAN YOU DISCOVER FROM MY FRIENDS BELOW **HOW** WE NAME POINTS?

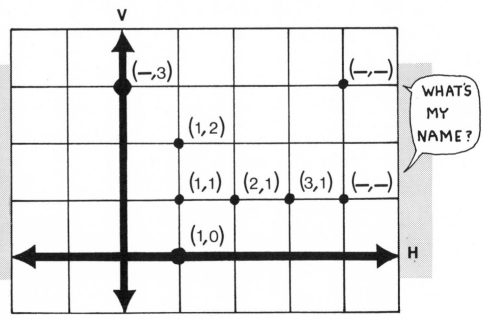

WHAT'S MY NAME?

(CONTINUED...)

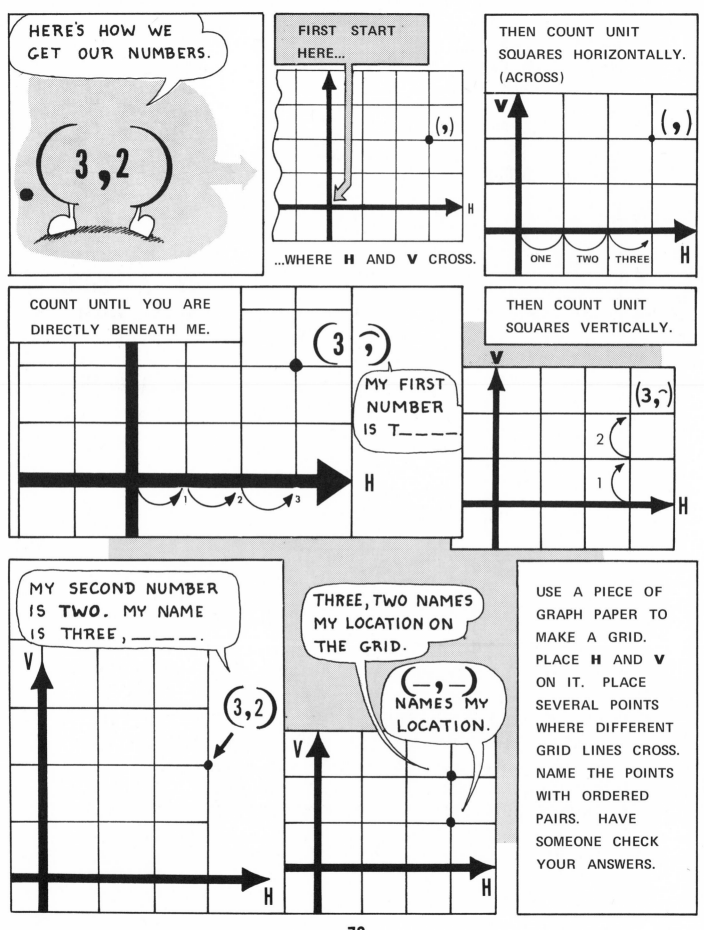

DIE PLOT GAME

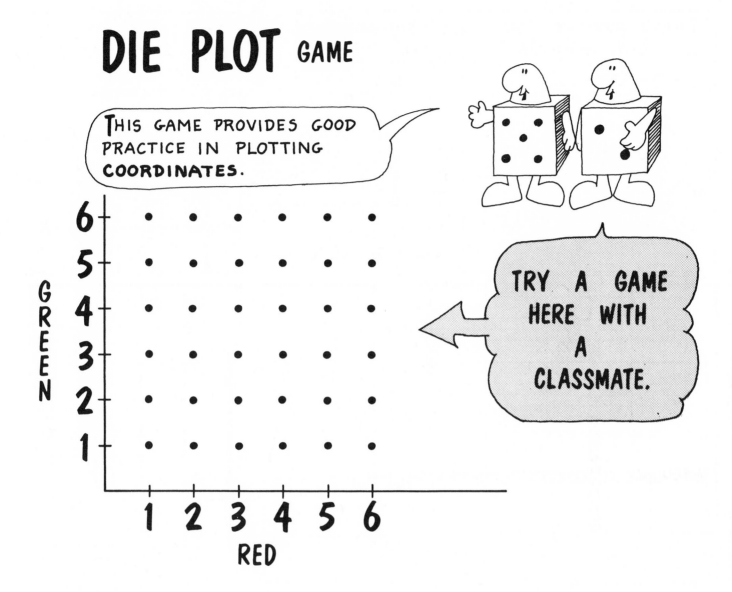

THIS GAME PROVIDES GOOD PRACTICE IN PLOTTING COORDINATES.

TRY A GAME HERE WITH A CLASSMATE.

1) DIE PLOT IS A GAME FOR TWO PEOPLE.
2) THE PLAYER THROWING THE HIGHEST TOTAL ON THE DICE STARTS THE GAME.
3) THE FIRST PLAYER ROLLS FOUR DICE — TWO RED, TWO GREEN. FROM THE FOUR, HE CHOOSES ONE RED AND ONE GREEN——— MARKING THE POINT THEY REPRESENT.
4) ONE PLAYER CIRCLES HIS POINT; THE OTHER X'S HIS.
5) ONCE A POINT IS COVERED, IT BELONGS TO THAT PLAYER.
6) FOUR IN A ROW WINS——— VERTICAL, HORIZONTAL OR DIAGONAL.

FATHER OF MODERN MATHEMATICS

THE IDEA OF COORDINATE SYSTEMS REPRESENTED A MERGING OF GEOMETRY AND ALGEBRA.

WHAT ARE YOU STARING AT?

ONE DAY HE WAS WATCHING A FLY CRAWLING ALONG THE CEILING OF HIS BEDROOM. HE GOT THE IDEA OF EXPRESSING THE MOTION OF THE FLY IN TERMS OF ITS DISTANCE FROM THE CORNER.

HE WAS ONE OF THE FIRST MATHEMATICIANS TO WRITE EQUATIONS WITH LETTERS AND SYMBOLS AS WE USE TODAY.

$3x + 2 = 14$

POINT
•

(X, Y)

LINE
$y = mx + 6$

CIRCLE
$O - r -$
$x^2 + y^2 = r^2$

HE WAS THE FIRST TO USE ALGEBRA TO STATE RULES FOR DRAWING CERTAIN GEOMETRICAL FIGURES.

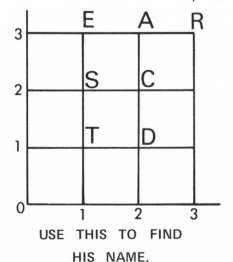

1596-1650

USE THIS TO FIND HIS NAME.

$\overline{\text{2,1}}$ $\overline{\text{1,3}}$ $\overline{\text{1,2}}$ $\overline{\text{2,2}}$ $\overline{\text{2,3}}$ $\overline{\text{3,3}}$ $\overline{\text{1,1}}$ $\overline{\text{1,3}}$ $\overline{\text{1,2}}$

PROPORTIONAL DRAWING

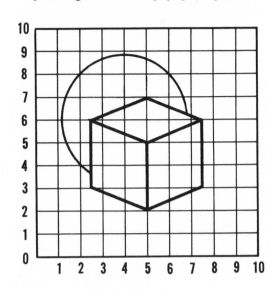

YOU CAN MAKE AN ENLARGEMENT OF THE DRAWING AT THE LEFT USING THE GRID BELOW.

PLACE ALL OF THE CORNERS OF THE CUBE ON THE SAME CORRESPONDING POINTS BELOW...THEN CONNECT THE POINTS.

THE EDGES OF THE CUBE YOU DRAW SHOULD BE TWICE THE LENGTH OF THE EDGES IN THE FIGURE ABOVE.

TRUE.

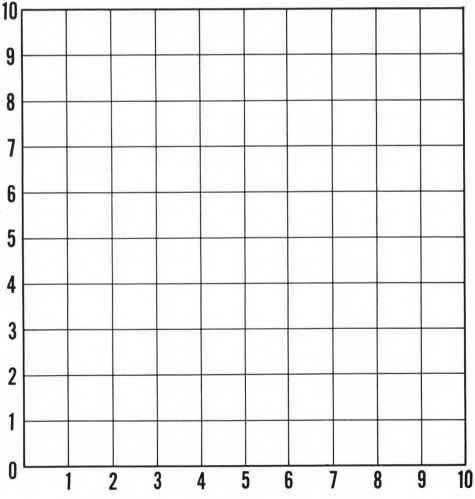

75

ORDER SORTER

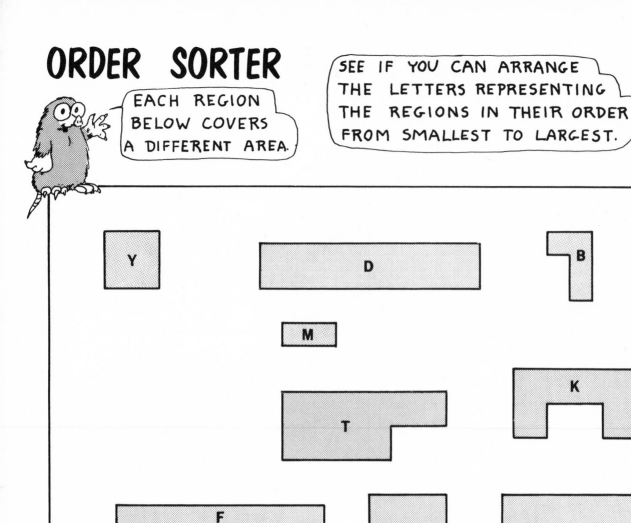

EACH REGION BELOW COVERS A DIFFERENT AREA.

SEE IF YOU CAN ARRANGE THE LETTERS REPRESENTING THE REGIONS IN THEIR ORDER FROM SMALLEST TO LARGEST.

$\underset{S}{M} < \underset{U}{B} < \underset{R}{Y} < \underset{P}{F} < \underset{R}{K} < \underset{S}{B} < \underset{S}{D} < \underset{E}{J}$

 SMALLEST REGION

 LARGEST REGION

USE THIS CHART TO DECODE THE LETTERS IN YOUR ANSWER.

A	B	C	D	E	F	G	H	I	J	K	L	M	N	O	P	Q	R	S	T	U	V	W	X	Y	Z
G	U	O	S	C	P	K	X	M	E	R	Y	S	T	H	V	L	A	W	I	D	N	Y	Z	R	F

— — — — — — — —

PROFILE PUZZLE
FIND THE CORRECT SIDE VIEW OF EACH FIGURE.

WHAT'S MY WORD?

IN THESE PROBLEMS, LETTERS HAVE REPLACED NUMBERS. BY STUDYING THE PROBLEMS CAN YOU FIND THE **CODE WORD?**

$$\overline{0 \quad 1 \quad 2 \quad 3 \quad 4 \quad 5 \quad 6 \quad 7 \quad 8 \quad 9}$$

```
  AM            AL           E
+ ON         x OM        A)DO
-----        -----        DO
  IN          ALM         ----
                           M
```

$$D \times D = D + D$$

```
  RAT
-  NO         LEND
-----       + AND        DONE
  TIL        -----     + ATOM       AND
             TOIL       -----     - ODD
                        NAME       -----
                                    RAM
```

78

A WHOLE THING

COMPLETE:

A ■ → **1**	E → **2/3**	I → ___	O → ___
B → **1/2**	F → ___	J → ___	P → ___
C → ___	G → ___	K → ___	Q → ___
D → ___	H → ___	L → ___	R → ___
		M → ___	S → ___
		N → ___	T → ___

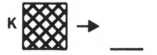

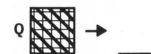

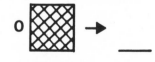
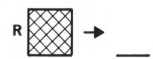

OPTICAL ILLUSIONS

DO THE SIDES OF THE "SQUARE" BEND INWARD? PLACE YOUR
FINGER IN THE CENTER OF THE PAGE AND MOVE THE PAGE
QUICKLY IN A CIRCULAR MOTION. CAN YOU SEE THE CIRCLES
TURN SEPARATELY? WHICH "BOXES" IN THE CENTER FIGURE
SEEM TO STAND OUT? WHICH "BOX" ON THE CORNER STANDS
OUT? CAN YOU ALWAYS BELIEVE WHAT YOU SEE?

THE LARGE SQUARE REPRESENTS ONE UNIT

C	B	A
C	C	
D	E	E	G H H I
F	F	E	J K I I
F	F	F	J K K I
			J K K L M

COMPLETE:

A = $\frac{1}{4}$ OF 1 = $\frac{1}{4}$

B = $\frac{1}{4}$ OF $\frac{1}{4}$ = $\frac{1}{16}$

C = $\frac{3}{4}$ OF $\frac{1}{4}$ = ___

D = ___ OF ___ = ___

E = ___ OF ___ = ___

F = ___ OF ___ = ___

G = ___ OF ___ = ___

H = ___ OF ___ = ___

I = ___ OF ___ = ___

J = ___ OF ___ = ___

K = ___ OF ___ = ___

L = ___ OF ___ OF ___ = ___

M = ___ OF ___ OF ___ = ___

COIN CAPERS

BOX O' DICE MAZE

KAREN CLARK, CLERK AT THE LOCAL TOY AND GAME SHOP, OPENED A BOX OF DICE. SHE "JUST HAPPENED TO NOTICE" THAT THERE WAS A "PATH" FROM THE UPPER LEFT—HAND CORNER TO THE LOWER RIGHT—HAND CORNER OF THE BOX. BY ALTERNATELY ADDING AND THEN SUBTRACTING, CAN YOU FIND THE PATH?

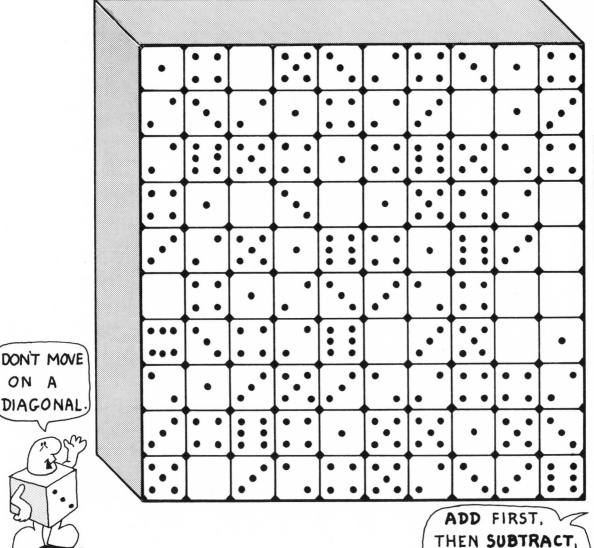

THE BLANK SPACES ACT AS ZEROS.

PASCAL'S TRIANGLE

THE TRIANGULAR ARRAY OF NUMBERS BELOW IS NAMED FOR A SEVENTEENTH CENTURY MATHEMATICIAN, BLAISE PASCAL. THE PATTERN CONTINUES WITHOUT AN END. CAN YOU FIND THE PATTERN AND FILL IN THE BLANKS BELOW?

1623-1662

BLAISE PASCAL

PATTERNS IN PASCAL'S TRIANGLE

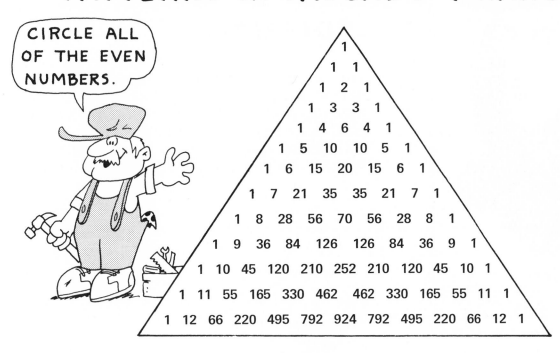

MORE PATTERNS IN PASCAL'S TRIANGLE

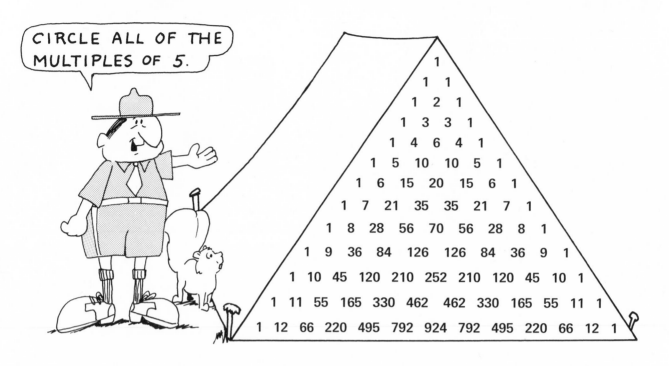

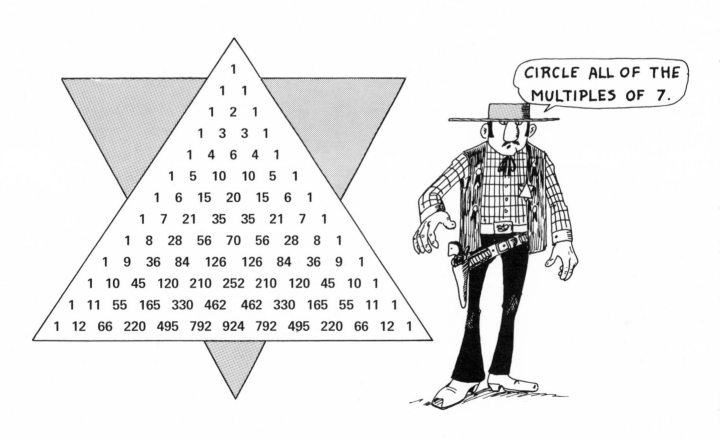

HOW MANY?

1

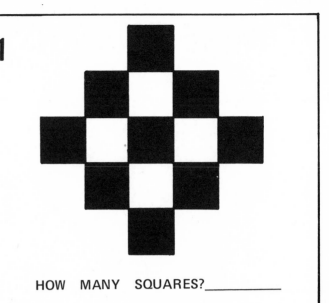

HOW MANY SQUARES? _____

2

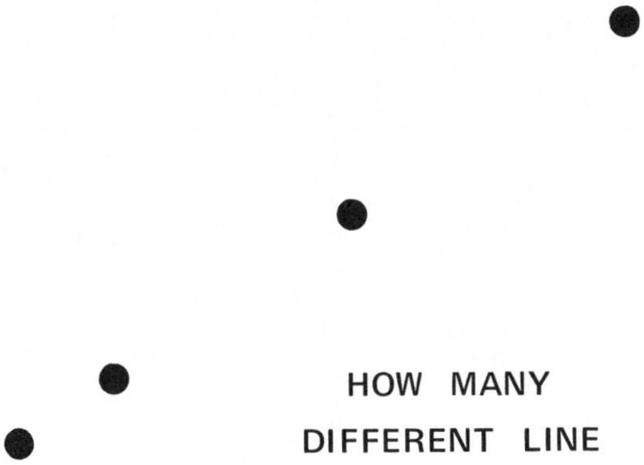

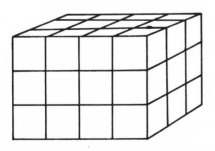

HOW MANY
DIFFERENT LINE
SEGMENTS?

_____

3

HOW MANY TRIANGLES?

_____

4

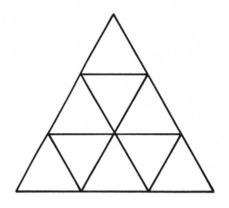

HOW MANY SMALL CUBES?

_____

COULD YOU HAVE SOLVED
PROBLEM TWO IF THERE
HAD BEEN ONE MORE DOT?

COULD YOU HAVE SOLVED
PROBLEM THREE IF THERE
HAD BEEN ONE MORE ROW
OF TRIANGLES?

UH!

LOGIC LURE

CINDY, DAWN AND
ZELMA ALL ATTEND
LEARNALOT SCHOOL.
THEY PRESENTLY HOLD
THE POSITIONS OF
CHEERLEADER, HEAD
TWIRLER AND STUDENT
BODY PRESIDENT, NOT
NECESSARILY IN THAT
ORDER.

LAST FRIDAY, THE TWIRLER LOOKED FOR HER FRIEND THE
PRESIDENT OF THE STUDENT BODY AFTER THE GAME, BUT
THE PRESIDENT HAD GONE OFF WITH THE CHEERLEADER.
THE PRESIDENT WAS CUTER THAN THE TWIRLER.
DAWN WAS CUTER THAN CINDY.
ZELMA HAD NEVER MET DAWN.

CAN YOU IDENTIFY EACH OF THE LOVELY GIRLS?

TANGRAMS

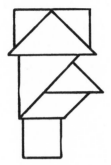

THE TANGRAM IS A WELL-KNOWN GEOMETRIC PUZ-
ZLE WHICH ORIGINATED LONG AGO. THE OBJECT IS
TO ASSEMBLE THE SEVEN PIECES SO AS TO FORM
VARIOUS FIGURES.   THE TANGRAM PIECES ARE
SHOWN IN THE DIAGRAM BELOW. USE THE PATTERN
TO MAKE YOUR OWN TANGRAM PUZZLE PIECES. CAN
YOU USE ALL SEVEN PIECES TO FORM THE FIGURES
SHOWN?

NUMBER SYSTEM

ABOUT 5,000 YEARS AGO A CHINESE PHILOSOPHER, **FO—HI**, WROTE **JE—KIM** (THE BOOK OF COMBINATIONS). THE BOOK CONTAINS A TABLE OF 63 LINE FIGURES. SOME OF THESE FIGURES ARE SHOWN BELOW. CAN YOU IDENTIFY THE MISSING NUMBERS?

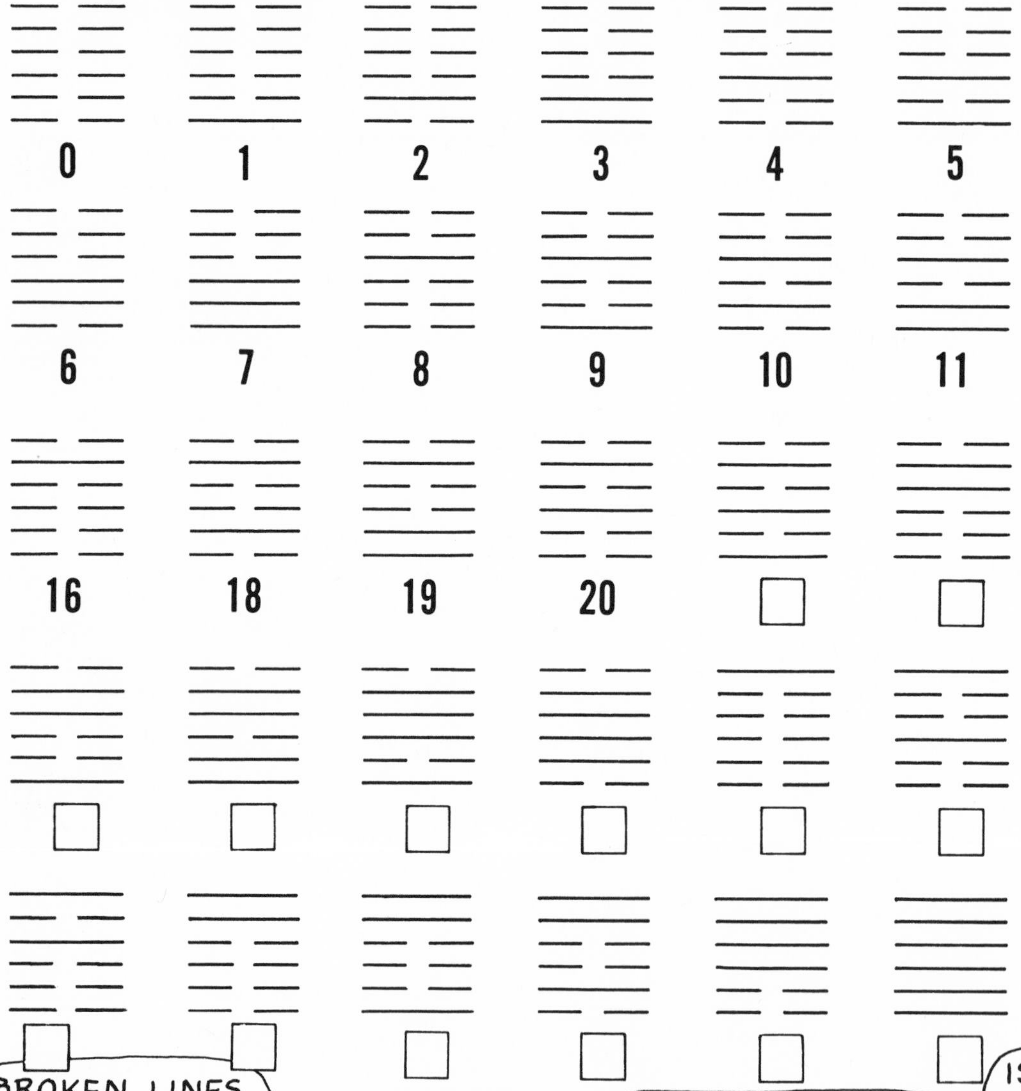

0   1   2   3   4   5

6   7   8   9   10   11

16   18   19   20   ☐   ☐

☐   ☐   ☐   ☐   ☐   ☐

☐   ☐   ☐   ☐   ☐   ☐

BROKEN LINES REPRESENT THE SYMBOL **0**.

CONTINUOUS LINES REPRESENT THE SYMBOL **1**.

ISN'T THIS JUST BASE TWO?

PROPORTIONAL DRAWING

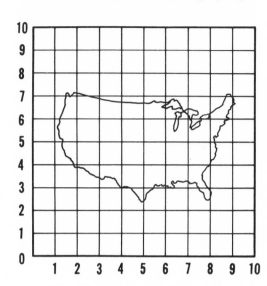

MAKE AN ENLARGEMENT OF THE DRAWING AT THE LEFT ON THE GRID BELOW

A LINE ON THE SMALL GRID SHOULD BE LOCATED ON A CORRESPONDING POSITION ON THE LARGE GRID.

THE AREA OF THE TWO DRAWINGS ARE IN THE RATIO OF 4 TO 1.

IF YOU DOUBLE THE DIMENSIONS YOU GET FOUR TIMES THE AREA.

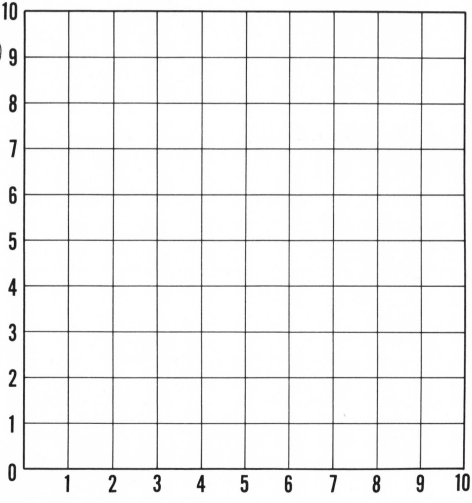

TILE TRIAL

USING ANY **THREE** OF THESE TILES, CAN YOU COMPLETE THE FOLLOWING SENTENCES?

EXAMPLE:

$$\boxed{4} \times \boxed{3} + \boxed{6} = 18$$

5

$$\boxed{} \times \boxed{} \div \boxed{} = 8$$

1

$$\boxed{} \times \boxed{} \div \boxed{} = 1$$

6

$$\boxed{} + \boxed{} + \boxed{} = 12$$

2

$$\boxed{} \times \boxed{} \div \boxed{} = 2$$

7

$$\boxed{} \times \boxed{} - \boxed{} = 14$$

3

$$\boxed{} \times \boxed{} - \boxed{} = 5$$

8

$$\boxed{} \times \boxed{} + \boxed{} = 15$$

4

$$\boxed{} \div \boxed{} \times \boxed{} = 6$$

CAN YOU GET SOME DIFFERENT ANSWERS USING ALL **FOUR** TILES?

FIT THE DISCS

ACROSS

AND

DOWN

COLORING MATH MAPS

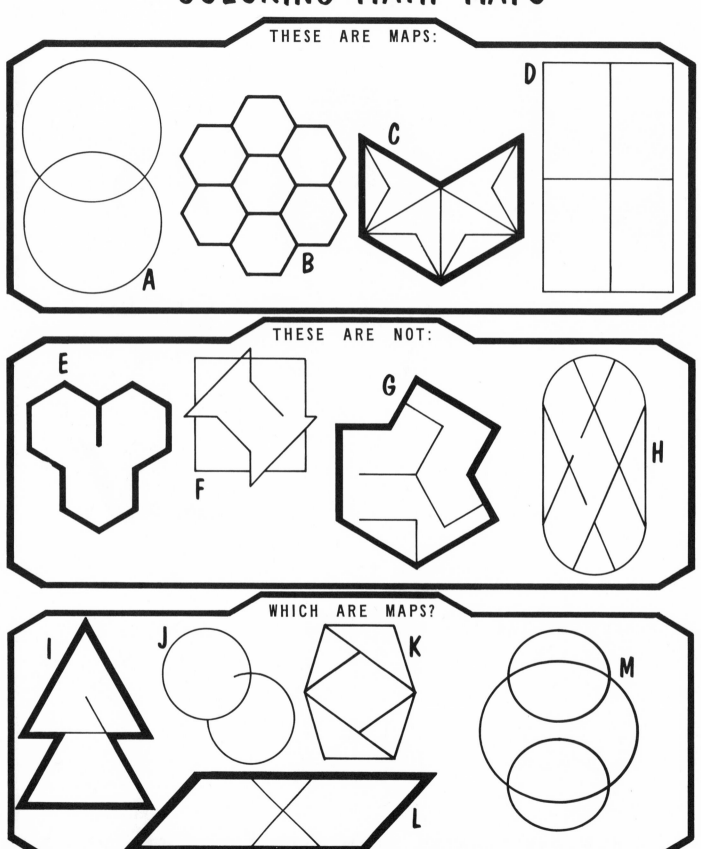

THESE ARE MAPS:

A B C D

THESE ARE NOT:

E F G H

WHICH ARE MAPS?

I J K L M

94

COLORING MATH MAPS

PROPERLY COLORED:

 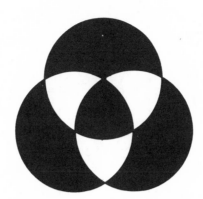 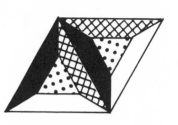

NOT PROPERLY COLORED:

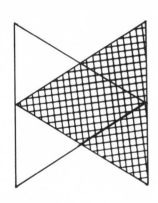 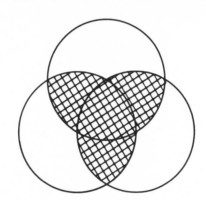 

PROPERLY COLOR THE MAPS ON THE PRECEEDING PAGE AND THOSE BELOW:

 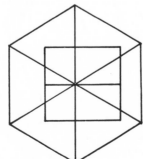 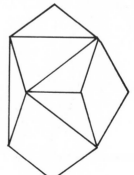

HOW MANY COLORS WERE NEEDED FOR EACH?

NAME GAME

H	O	N	E	I	T	G	O	O	G	O	L
U	N	E	I	G	H	T	S	E	V	E	N
N	D	R	E	F	O	U	R	T	T	S	T
Q	U	A	D	I	R	S	T	H	N	E	E
N	I	T	R	I	O	A	N	D	T	V	N
I	E	M	I	T	F	I	F	T	E	E	N
N	B	I	L	L	I	O	I	W	E	N	N
E	T	Y	T	S	V	N	F	E	T	T	E
T	E	N	H	I	E	F	T	L	G	H	T
Z	E	S	I	X	S	I	Y	V	H	S	E
E	R	O	R	T	E	F	T	E	T	N	E
F	O	R	T	Y	V	T	E	E	Y	I	N
O	U	R	Y	T	E	N	N	N	I	N	E
U	R	T	E	E	N	T	Y	I	N	E	S

HORIZONTAL,   VERTICAL,   OR ZIG-ZAG

96

PATTERN PICTURE

PLOTTING POINTS

GRAPH THE FOLLOWING POINTS AND CONNECT EACH POINT
WITH THE NEXT POINT USING STRAIGHT LINE SEGMENTS.

CONNECT :
(24,12),(14,29),(25,18),
(24,12),(14,2),(3,13),
(5,19),(14,29),(3,13)
AND (24,12)

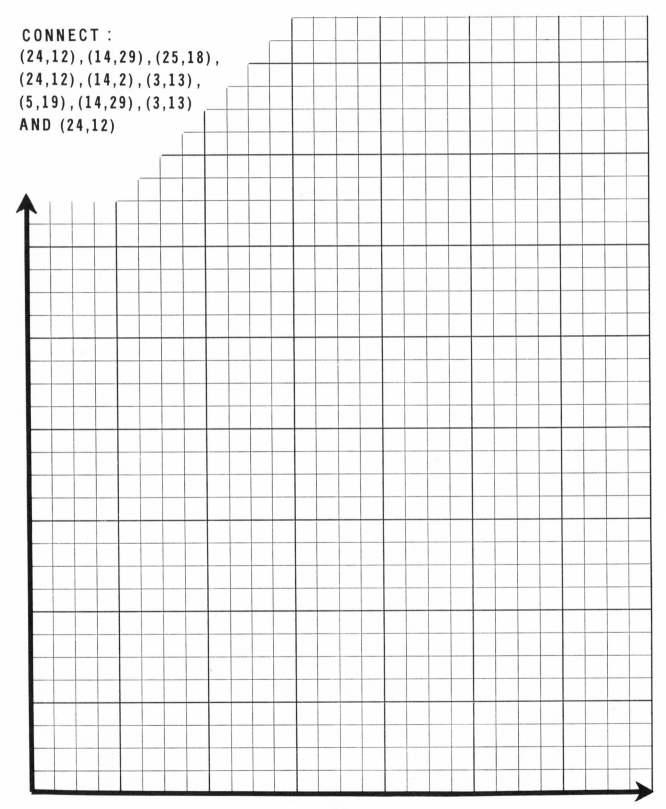

ACCURACY

IN ORDER TO GET THE CORRECT SUM TO THE ADDITION PROBLEM BELOW, YOU MUST DO MORE THAN 60 ADDITIONS. ONE MISTAKE WILL RESULT IN A WRONG ANSWER. HOW IS YOUR ACCURACY? CAN YOU FIND THE CORRECT SUM THE FIRST TIME?

```
  72403916
  85992104
  17374558
  60239768
  48963217
  51827584
  36750831
+ 82397259
_____
```

99

PHOTO ALBUM PAGES

CAN YOU PLACE THESE SNAPSHOTS ON THE PHOTO ALBUM PAGES?

1

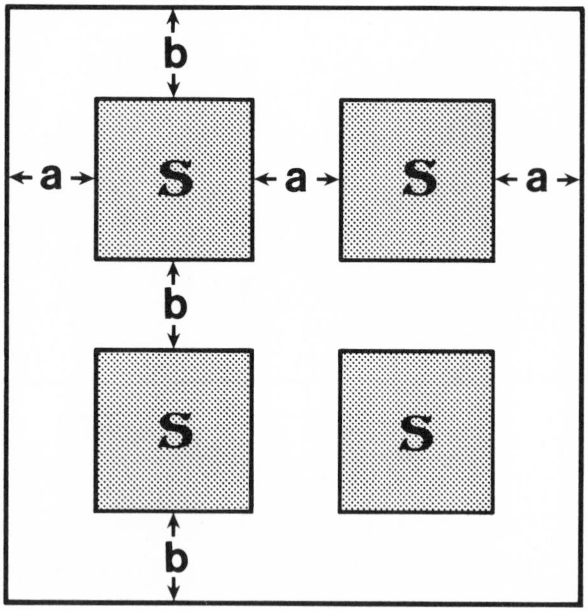
b
a
S
a
S
a
b
S
S
b

1. Album page: 33 cm x 33 cm
   S: 9 cm x 9 cm
   Find: a = _____ cm, b = _____ cm

2

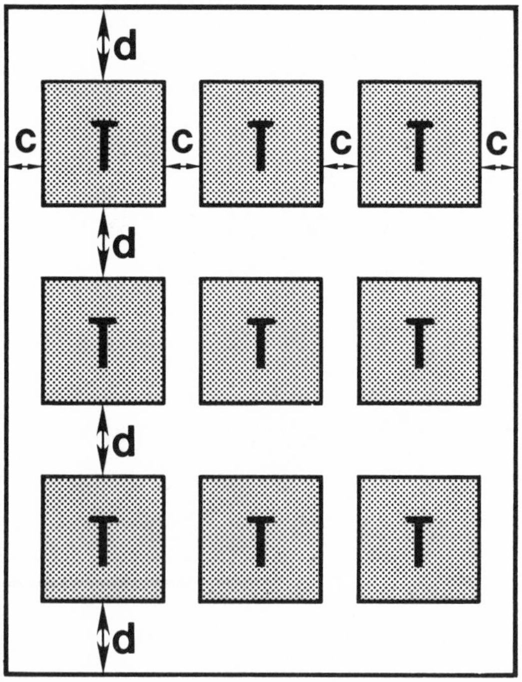
d
c
T
c
T
c
T
c
d
T
T
T
d
T
T
T
d

2. Album page: 29 cm x 37 cm
   T: 7 cm x 7 cm
   Find: c = _____ cm, d = _____ cm

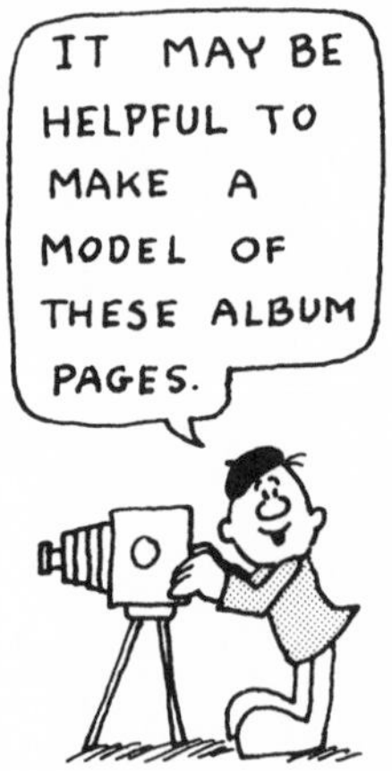
IT MAY BE HELPFUL TO MAKE A MODEL OF THESE ALBUM PAGES.

3

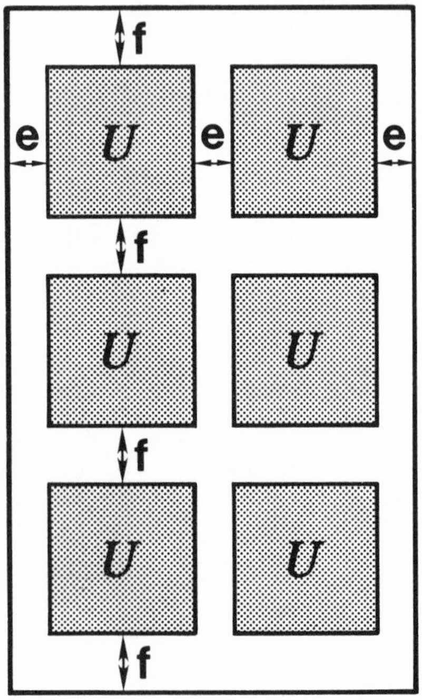
f
e
U
e
U
e
f
U
U
f
U
U
f

3. Album page: 11 in. x 18 in.
   U: 4 in. x 4 in.
   Find: e = _____ in., f = _____ in.

PHOTO ALBUM PAGES

CAN YOU PLACE THESE SNAPSHOTS
ON THE PHOTO ALBUM PAGES?

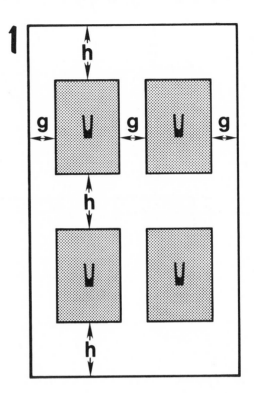

1. Album page: 24 cm x 39 cm

   V: 7.5 cm x 10.5 cm

   Find: g = _____ cm, h = _____ cm

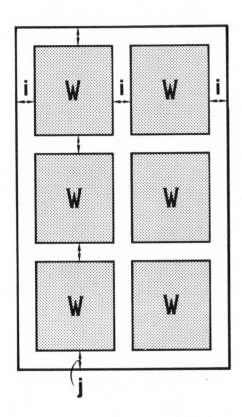

2. Album page: 12 in. x 19 in.

   W: $4\frac{1}{2}$ in. wide x 5 in. high

   Find: i = _____ in., j = _____ in.

3. Album page: 30 cm x 38 cm

   X: 6 cm x 10 cm

   Find: k = _____ cm, l = _____ cm,

   m = _____ cm

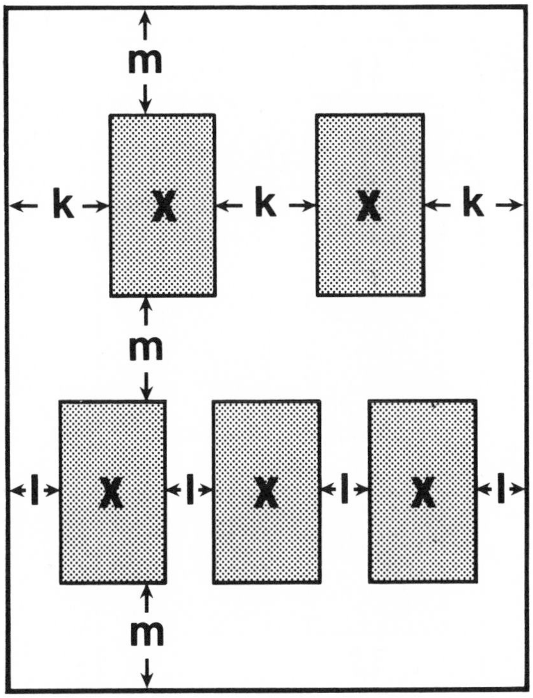

JANE HAS:

PENNIES, NICKELS, AND DIMES IN HER PURSE.

SHE HAS EIGHT COINS ALTOGETHER, INCLUDING

MORE DIMES THAN NICKELS,

MORE NICKELS THAN PENNIES, AND

FEWER PENNIES THAN NICKELS.

WHAT ARE THE TWO DIFFERENT AMOUNTS OF MONEY SHE COULD HAVE?

COMPUTATION RELAY

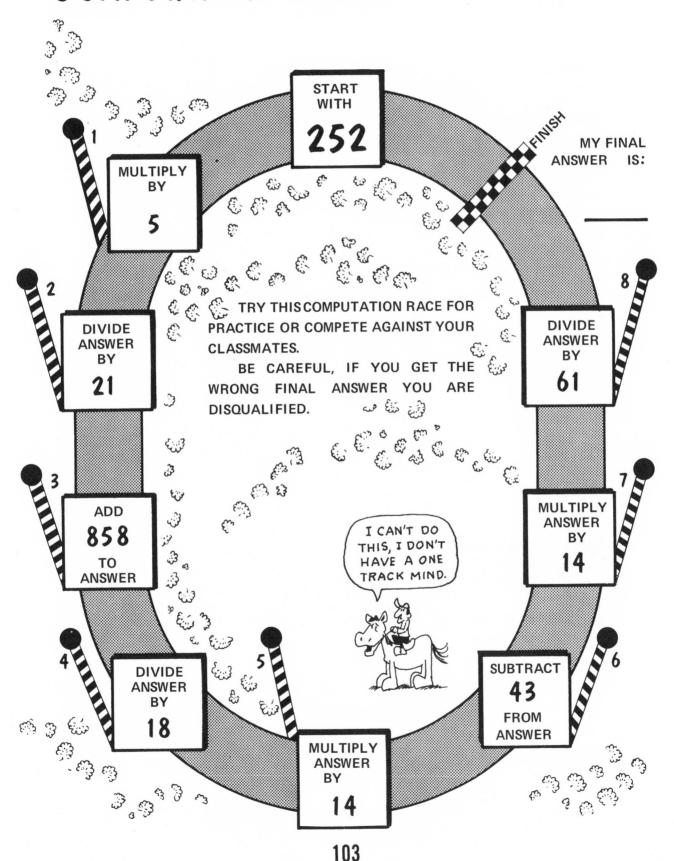

START WITH
252

FINISH

MY FINAL ANSWER IS: _____

1 MULTIPLY BY **5**

2 DIVIDE ANSWER BY **21**

3 ADD **858** TO ANSWER

4 DIVIDE ANSWER BY **18**

5 MULTIPLY ANSWER BY **14**

6 SUBTRACT **43** FROM ANSWER

7 MULTIPLY ANSWER BY **14**

8 DIVIDE ANSWER BY **61**

TRY THIS COMPUTATION RACE FOR PRACTICE OR COMPETE AGAINST YOUR CLASSMATES.

BE CAREFUL, IF YOU GET THE WRONG FINAL ANSWER YOU ARE DISQUALIFIED.

I CAN'T DO THIS, I DON'T HAVE A ONE TRACK MIND.

103

Random Digit Activities

I. SUM IT UP

Find the sum of a column of one digit numbers on the random digit page. For example,

1	5	9
6	8	0
7,	13,	3
		4
		16.

Within a time limit of five or ten minutes, compete to find 1) the greatest number of complete problems, or 2) the highest total of sums. Players should be able to describe the location of a total using the grid coordinates to locate the units' digit in the sum. All players should check the winner's answer.

VARIATION: Find the differences. Subtract adjacent single digit numbers in a column.

II. TWENTY-ONE

On the random digit page circle chains of numbers that total 21. A number chain is a row (horizontal) or a column (vertical) of adjacent numbers. In this activity, numbers on a diagonal also make a number chain but corners do not. For example,

OK   NO

VARIATIONS: a) Choose a different total number.
b) Accept only column number chains.
c) Accept only row number chains.

III. DIGIT BINGO

Draw a border around a square of 25 digits to use as a Bingo card. A caller spins a 1-10 spinner and calls out the number pointed to. Circle all number chains on the card that total that number. You may extend a circle outside the card boundaries if necessary but no numbers can be circled more than once. The first player to circle all numbers on the card wins.

See other random digit sheets and games in *Aftermath II and III.* Create your own random digit sheet and use it to play these games or games you make up.

RANDOM DIGIT PAGE

	1	2	3	4	5	6	7	8	9	10	11	12	13	14	15	16	17	18	19	20
25	1	7	2	5	8	2	1	4	6	1	5	7	2	9	8	0	7	4	9	6
24	9	0	3	6	1	4	7	5	0	7	9	4	5	6	5	1	6	2	5	8
23	6	4	5	9	3	0	8	1	9	3	8	1	0	3	7	0	4	9	3	1
22	1	3	2	5	4	6	2	7	4	6	2	9	6	2	8	7	2	6	4	9
21	4	9	0	3	1	9	3	0	8	0	1	5	3	8	1	9	5	1	6	3
20	7	5	4	2	8	7	5	9	2	9	4	6	1	0	7	3	8	2	0	5
19	0	2	7	3	5	0	2	7	3	1	7	0	8	5	6	0	7	4	9	2
18	5	6	1	7	4	8	4	0	6	4	2	9	7	3	4	2	9	8	5	4
17	1	4	8	0	6	2	9	5	3	4	8	3	8	0	8	5	1	6	1	7
16	3	9	2	7	1	8	1	2	6	1	7	0	4	9	1	8	3	2	7	8
15	8	0	8	3	6	4	8	5	0	8	3	5	9	6	3	0	7	4	3	6
14	2	7	1	7	0	5	7	8	4	2	7	1	3	7	5	9	6	0	5	2
13	8	3	6	4	7	2	0	1	6	8	9	4	0	5	2	4	1	8	2	9
12	9	2	5	1	8	9	3	9	0	5	0	6	1	9	7	5	8	3	7	4
11	0	6	8	9	2	6	7	4	2	6	3	9	2	0	6	0	9	0	8	1
10	7	4	0	7	4	1	3	5	1	9	2	6	4	3	1	7	4	6	5	9
9	2	3	8	1	8	6	0	3	4	0	7	1	6	0	5	2	9	8	1	7
8	6	5	3	9	3	5	2	9	6	5	2	8	3	9	4	7	3	5	9	3
7	3	1	6	1	8	2	4	1	3	7	4	7	5	0	8	0	6	8	2	8
6	8	0	4	2	5	3	1	5	4	0	9	2	6	3	7	9	3	1	7	5
5	4	6	3	7	0	8	0	6	2	5	3	1	4	8	5	2	8	6	4	8
4	1	4	5	4	9	5	6	3	9	1	7	0	6	7	0	6	4	5	9	2
3	7	3	1	6	2	7	4	1	0	6	3	2	5	3	9	1	7	0	1	6
2	5	9	2	8	0	3	5	2	7	4	9	4	0	8	4	6	3	8	2	9
1	0	7	4	2	6	1	8	9	3	5	1	6	9	5	2	7	0	9	8	4

DIGIT DISCOVERY

WHAT DIGIT IS UNDER EACH PANCAKE BELOW?

NUMBERS 1-9 EACH APPEAR UNDER THE PANCAKES.

FOUR CORNERS ARE ODD NUMBERS.

ROW 1 CONTAINS THREE CONSECUTIVE ODD NUMBERS.

ONE OF THE DIAGONALS CONTAINS PRIME FACTORS OF 84.

NUMBERS IN ROW 1 ARE FACTORS OF 30.

COLUMN 3 TOTAL IS TWICE ROW 1 TOTAL.

COLUMN 1 TOTAL EQUALS ROW 3 TOTAL.

NUMBERS IN COLUMN 1 ARE FACTORS OF 72.

COLUMN 1　COLUMN 2　COLUMN 3

ROW 1

ROW 2

ROW 3

SOLUTIONS

BOOK ONE

ABACUS, Page 3

D O   Y O U   T R U S T   P L U S
O N   A B A C U S

WHICH ONE DIFFERS?, Page 4

A) 2   B) 3   C) 4   D) 5   E) 4

MATH PUN FUN, Page 5

H A L F, W H O L E, E I G H T,
D E C I M A L, F R A C T I O N

E I G H T
1 2 3 4 5

SEVEN SUM PUZZLE, Page 8

| 4 | 5 | = 9 | | 5 | 6 | = 11 | | 9 | 7 | = 16 |

4	5	6
9	7	8
13	12	14

| 7 | 8 | = 15 |

Samples from the 36 solutions:

1	2	3	2	1	3	3	1	2
6	4	5	6	5	4	5	6	4

GUESSTIMATES, Pages 9–12

dots – 600, miles – 20, ducks – 150,
tally marks – 500

A) 36 B) 96 C) 55 D) 46 E) 45 F) 60

EVEN AND ODD, Page 13

+	O	E
O	E	O
E	O	E

X	O	E
O	O	E
E	E	E

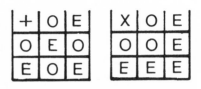

ODD AND EVEN MAZE, Page 14

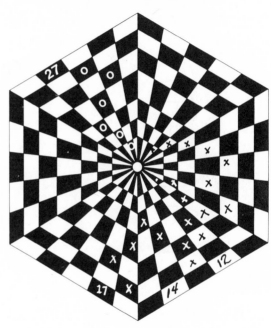

ADD–SUB SLIDE RULE, Page 19

The chart shown below is not a square because the sum of certain elements has been left un-defined.

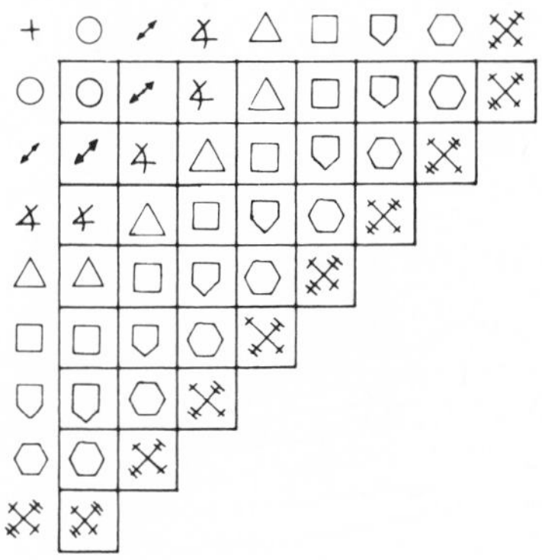

TOWERS OF POWERS, Page 22

A	B	C	D
$1^0 = 1$	$2^0 = 1$	$3^0 = 1$	$4^0 = 1$
$1^1 = 1$	$2^1 = 2$	$3^1 = 3$	$4^1 = 4$
$1^2 = 1$	$2^2 = 4$	$3^2 = 9$	$4^2 = 16$
$1^3 = 1$	$2^3 = 8$	$3^3 = 27$	$4^3 = 64$
$1^4 = 1$	$2^4 = 16$	$3^4 = 81$	$4^4 = 256$
$1^5 = 1$	$2^5 = 32$		

STAR SEARCH, Page 23

1) 7 2) 6 3) 1 4) 4 5) 5 6) 2 7) 3

PUZZLERS, Page 25

The order of finish was: A D C E B

The next square year will be the year 2025.

1 2 1 1 1

Pour glass 4 into glass 1 and replace glass 4.

DOT – DOT – DOT . . ., Page 26

1) 1, 2, 3, 4, . . ., 98, 99, 100

2) 0, 1, 2, 3, . . ., 76, 77, 78, 79

3) 0, 2, 4, 6, . . ., 194, 196, 198

4) 1, 3, 5, 7, . . ., 75, 77, 79

TINKERTOTALS, Page 29

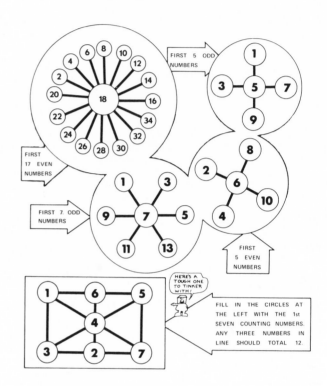

TILE TRIAL, Page 31

Answers not unique

1) $6 - 4 - 2 = 0$ 5) $3 - 2 + 4 = 5$

2) $3 + 2 - 4 = 1$ 6) $6 + 4 - 3 = 7$

3) $4 + 2 - 3 = 3$ 7) $6 + 4 - 2 = 8$

4) $6 + 2 - 4 = 4$ 8) $4 + 3 + 2 = 9$

GREAT MATHEMATICIAN, Page 33

N E W T O N

1 2 3 4 5 6

SHAPES QUIZ, Page 34

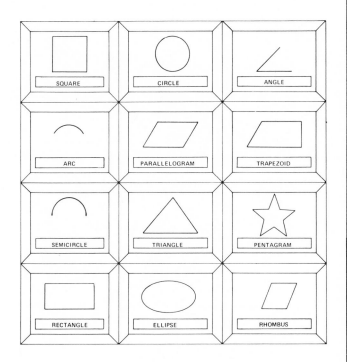

SQUARE UNITS, Page 35

2) 6   3) yes   4) 1   5) yes
6) 1   7) yes   8) 1 ½ 9) 2 ½

SQUARE UNITS, Page 36

A) 2 sq. units   D) 10½ sq. units
B) 4 sq. units   E) 17 sq. units
C) 3 sq. units   F) 9 sq. units

LINE DESIGN, Page 37

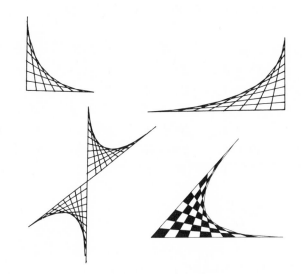

13 PATTERNS, Page 38

All patterns except D, H, K and M
fold into an open box.

DIVISIBILITY, Page 39

Circle numbers divisible by 2: 162; 4,560;
    24,986; 39,604; 82,588
Divisible by 2: B, C, D, G, J

DIVISIBILITY, Page 40

Sum of digits: A) 10   B) 6   C) 12
        D) 18   E) 15   F) 29
Numbers divisible by 3: A, C, E, G, and I

DIVISIBILITY, Page 41

Divisible by 4: A, D, and E
Divisible by 5: 8 3 2 6 4 4 5 9 2 0; 5 0 0 0 0 5;
        26040   35   895   630   3745

DIVISIBILITY, Page 42

Numbers divisible by 2 and 3:

A) 12, 24, 96, 132, 570, 275310

B) 18, 48, 84, 4506, 23610, 625430789173554

C) 54, 96.

A number divisible by six is divisible by 2 and 3.

MATH GOLF, Page 43

$2 + 2 + 2 + 2 + 3 + 3 + 2 + 3 + 4 = 23$ (low total)

3 X 3 X 3 CUBE, Page 44

8,   12,   6,   1

HOW MANY ?, Page 45

1) 14   2) 18   3) 6   4) 24

General solutions:

1) $1^2 + 2^2 + \ldots + (n - 1)^2 + n^2$

3) $\dfrac{n(n - 1)}{2}$

4) $n !$

ATTRIBUTES, Page 47

B) 7   C) 2   D) both have bands

E) 8 and 12   F) 4   G) 3 and 6

H) Same shape, color and a feather. No band.

MAZE, Page 48

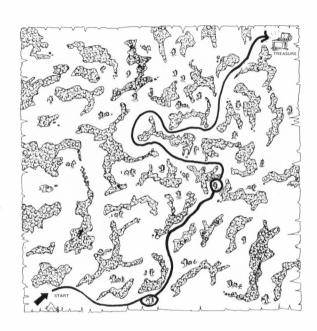

MULTIPLE MADNESS, Page 50

30 YEARS	—	2,000
60 YEARS	—	4,000
90 YEARS	—	8,000
120 YEARS	—	16,000
150 YEARS	—	32,000
180 YEARS	—	64,000
210 YEARS	—	128,000
240 YEARS	—	256,000
270 YEARS	—	512,000
300 YEARS	—	1,024,000

LOGIC, Pages 53—54

1) 4   2) 3   3) 2   4) 5   5) 3   6) 4

1) 1   2) 3   3) 5   4) 4   5) 3   6) 1   7) 1

HEX NUMBER PUZZLE, Page 55

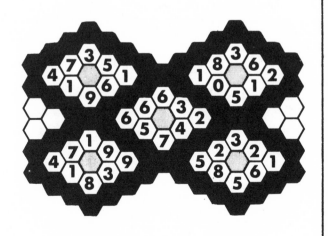

ARROWMATH, Page 57

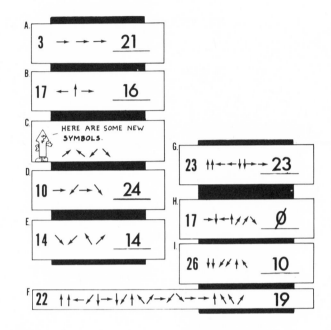

WHICH ONE DIFFERS?, Page 58

A) 4   B) 5   C) 4   D) 5   E) 5

TRIANGLE THEOREM, Page 59

A TRIANGLE CAN POSSESS AT MOST ONE RIGHT ANGLE.

MOVING MATCHES, Page 60

1)

MOVING MATCHES, Page 60 (cont.)

2)

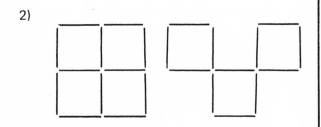

3)   V = IV + I

4)   Rotate paper 180 degrees.

WHICH ONE DIFFERS?, Page 61

Number 9 differs.

PATTERNS AND SEQUENCES, Page 62

1) 1 2 3 4 5 6 7

2) 2 4 6 8 10 12 14

3) 7 11 15 19 23 27 31

4) 1 2 4 8 16 32 64

5) 1 4 9 16 25 36 49

6) 1 3 5 7 9 11 13

7) 0 4 8 12 16 20 24

8) 1 10 100 10³ 10⁴ 10⁵ 10⁶

9) 2 3 5 7 11 13 17

10) 1 1 2 3 5 8 13

MULTIPLE MAZE, Page 64

7	14	20	27	54	61	76	83
13	21	27	44	55	63	70	77
20	28	35	42	49	56	90	84
27	34	41	48	55	62	97	91
160	153	146	139	132	125	104	98
154	147	140	133	126	119	112	105
161	167	188	195	202	227	216	111
168	175	182	189	196	203	210	217

3	2	5	6	13	17	37	58	59	64
6	4	14	7	16	19	35	61	62	65
9	12	15	18	20	22	32	67	68	70
11	8	10	21	23	31	66	69	72	75
33	30	27	24	25	34	63	73	71	78
36	28	26	29	30	74	60	94	95	81
39	42	45	48	51	54	57	93	87	84
38	40	41	47	76	77	78	80	90	97
43	44	46	49	85	83	79	87	93	92
50	52	53	56	86	89	88	91	96	99

9	17	26	71	107	162	171	180
18	28	53	62	161	153	188	189
27	36	45	55	152	144	197	198
26	44	54	62	143	135	206	207
35	71	63	73	125	126	215	216
89	80	72	82	109	117	125	225
98	91	81	90	99	108	118	234
107	100	89	98	107	116	127	243

PRIME TIME, Page 65

CIRCULAR REASONING MAZE, Page 66

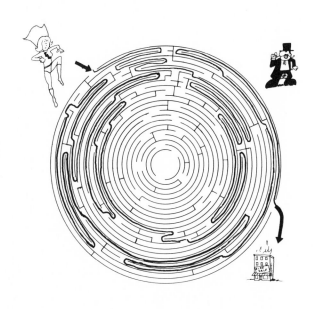

AVERAGES, Page 67

Average hat size: 7
Average age: 22
Average height: 62 inches

TRELLIS TWISTER, Page 68

Number 8.

DIJAKNOWTHAT, Page 69

8, 999, 991

FATHER OF MODERN MATHEMATICS, Page 74

D E S C A R T E S
(2,1) (1,3) (1,2) (2,2) (2,3) (3,3) (1,1) (1,3) (1,2)

ORDER SORTER, Page 76

M < B < Y < F < K < T < D < J
S   U   R   P   R   I   S   E

PROFILE PUZZLE, Page 77

A) 5   B) 2   C) 4   D) 3

WHAT'S MY WORD?, Page 78

M O D E L   T R A I N

A WHOLE THING, Page 79

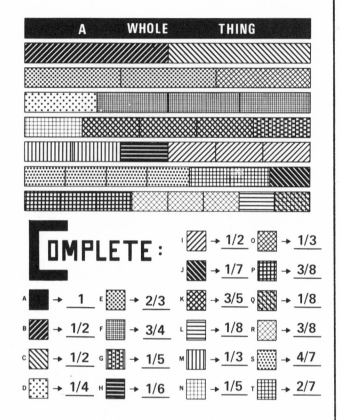

COMPLETE:

| I | → 1/2 | O | → 1/3 |
| J | → 1/7 | P | → 3/8 |

A	→ 1	E	→ 2/3	K	→ 3/5	Q	→ 1/8
B	→ 1/2	F	→ 3/4	L	→ 1/8	R	→ 3/8
C	→ 1/2	G	→ 1/5	M	→ 1/3	S	→ 4/7
D	→ 1/4	H	→ 1/6	N	→ 1/5	T	→ 2/7

LARGE SQUARE REPRESENTS ONE
  UNIT, Page 81

A = 1/4 of 1 = 1/4   H = 1/8 of 1/4 = 1/32

B = 1/4 of 1/4 = 1/16   I = 1/4 of 1/4 = 1/16

C = 3/4 of 1/4 = 3/16   J = 3/16 of 1/4 = 3/64

D = 1/9 of 1/4 = 1/36   K = 5/16 of 1/4 = 5/64

E = 1/3 of 1/4 = 1/12   L = 1/9 of 1/16 of

F = 5/9 of 1/4 = 5/36   1/4 = 1/576

G = 1/16 of 1/4 = 1/64   M = 8/9 of 1/16 of

                                1/4 = 1/72

COIN CAPERS, Page 82

A) Move penny or dime to the other end.

B) Six pennies. Three pennies form an
    equilateral triangle.

C)

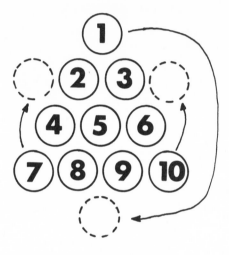

BOX O' DICE MAZE, Page 83

1 + 2 = 3; 3 − 2 = 1; 1 + 4 = 5;
5 − 0 = 5; 5 + 1 = 6; etc.

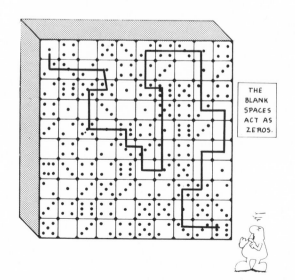

THE
BLANK
SPACES
ACT AS
ZEROS.

PASCAL'S TRIANGLE, Page 84

PATTERNS IN PASCAL'S TRIANGLE,
Pages 85–86

PASCAL'S TRIANGLE, Page 85

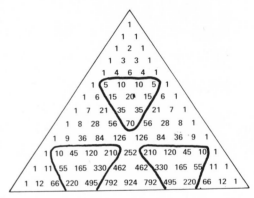

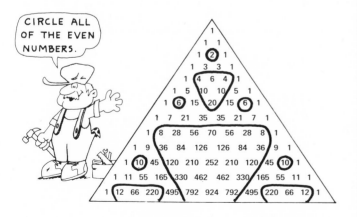

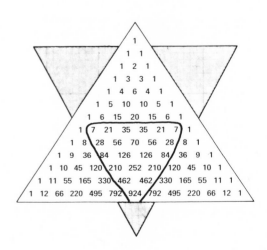

HOW MANY?, Page 87

1) 18   2) 6   3) 13   4) 36

LOGIC LURE, Page 88

Cindy — cheerleader
Dawn — president
Zelma — twirler

TANGRAMS, Page 89

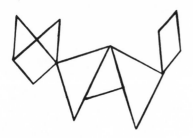

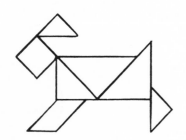

TANGRAMS, Page 89 (cont.)

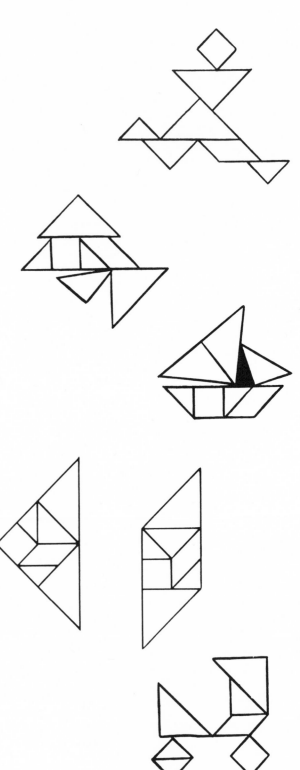

NUMBER SYSTEM, Page 90

0	1	2	3	4	5
6	7	8	9	10	11
16	18	19	20	21	24
25	27	29	30	32	36
40	48	49	50	60	63

TILE TRIAL, Page 92

1) $2 \times 3 \div 6 = 1$ 5) $6 \times 4 \div 3 = 8$

2) $3 \times 4 \div 6 = 2$ 6) $6 + 4 + 2 = 12$

3) $2 \times 4 - 3 = 5$ 7) $6 \times 3 - 4 = 14$

4) $4 \div 2 \times 3 = 6$ 8) $2 \times 6 + 3 = 15$

Answers not unique

FIT THE DISCS, Page 93

$$5 \times 4 \div 2 = 10$$
$$\times \quad + \quad +$$
$$6 \times 9 \div 3 = 18$$
$$\div \quad - \quad +$$
$$5 + 7 - 8 = 4$$
$$= \quad = \quad =$$
$$6 \quad 6 \quad 13$$

$$10 - 7 - 1 = 2$$
$$- \quad + \quad +$$
$$5 + 9 - 3 = 11$$
$$- \quad - \quad -$$
$$4 + 6 + 2 = 12$$
$$= \quad = \quad =$$
$$1 \quad 10 \quad 2$$

Answers not unique

COLORING MATH MAPS, Pages 94–95

These are maps. Colors needed: 3, 3, 3

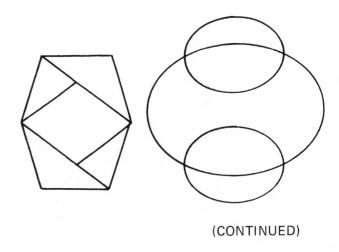

(CONTINUED)

117

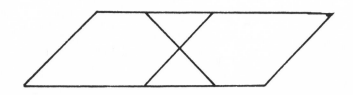

NAME GAME, Page 96

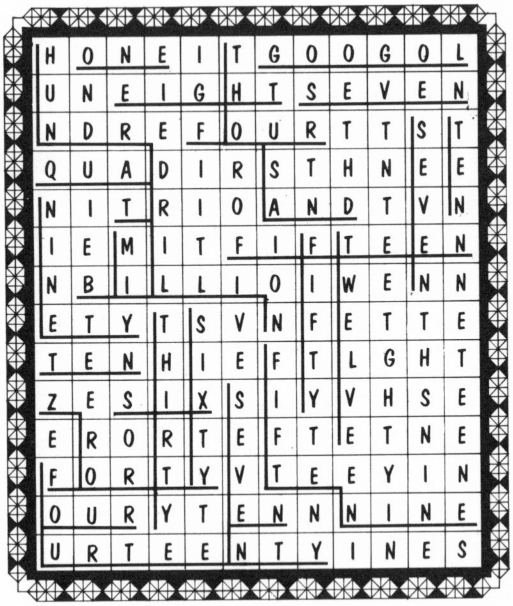

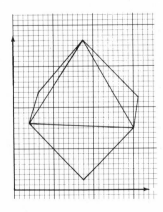

PLOTTING POINTS, Page 98

ACCURACY, Page 99

455, 949, 237

PHOTO ALBUM PAGES, Page 100

1. a = 5 cm, b = 5 cm
2. c = 2 cm, d = 4 cm
3. e = 1 in., f = 1.5 in.

PHOTO ALBUM PAGES, Page 101

1. g = 3 cm, h = 6 cm
2. i = 1 in., j = 1 in.
3. k = 6 cm, l = 3 cm, m = 6 cm

JANE HAS, Page 102

61¢; 1 penny, 2 nickels, 5 dimes
56¢; 1 penny, 3 nickels, 4 dimes

COMPUTATION RELAY, Page 103
154

DIGIT DISCOVERY, Page 106

3	1	5
8	2	6
9	4	7

INDEX

INDEX